TOUGH/NICE

A Manager's Guide to Sustained High Performance

Shale & Candace Paul

DELTA GROUP PRESS
Evergreen, Colorado

DELTA GROUP PRESS
Box 40
Evergreen, Colorado 80439

PRINTED IN THE UNITED STATES OF AMERICA

*Cover by Richard M. Kohen, Shadow Canyon Graphics,
Evergreen, Colorado*

*This book was typeset by Don Council of Desktop
Publishing & Printing using VENTURA Publisher.*

Desktop Publishing & Printing
*225 Mariposa
Denver, CO 80223
(303) 623-5757*

Table of Contents

ACKNOWLEDGEMENTS

As you read this book, you will observe there are virtually no footnotes or references to other source material, nor is there a lengthy bibliography from which the information from this book was gathered. There is a reason for these omissions. The observations, approaches, steps, and illustrations were developed from our own experience. To a significant degree, we have reported our own learnings. Since most of the insights were gained by trial and error in many different situations and over time, there is no one great teacher to thank. Yet, without the many and varied interactions and relationships along the way, this book would not have been possible. We thank, therefore, those people with whom we have been privileged to work who, by design or inadvertence, have taught us so much. It is probably fair to say that, at the time, their contributions were not always recognized or even welcome. In retrospect, however, their value has been immense.

We do want to thank certain individuals who were gracious and dedicated enough to take their time to read the manuscript drafts and offer their helpful and constructive comments: Mary Hey, our editor; and Steve Boeding, Dan Johnson, and Michael Lucibello, our readers. Thanks also to Don Council whose astute guidance in the computer area made the writing and assembly of this material much easier. Finally, a special vote of thanks to Max Wettstein, Candy's son, who assisted in designing the book cover.

Introduction

Peak performance and high achievement are popular management topics these days. Having exhausted the possibilities of concepts borrowed from the military, business is now turning to the world of sports for its lessons. This should not seem surprising, since many American firms have become copiers rather than innovators. New ideas in recent years have originated in Tokyo rather than Detroit, and capital in the form of adverse trade balances is moving from rather than toward the U.S. In major industries--autos, steel, high tech, and perhaps even space technology and weaponry--America is no longer the acknowledged leader. Too many American companies have become importers and imitators, rushing frantically to catch up in the race for economic superiority.

The current emphasis on peak performance is fine as far as it goes. But even the word "peak" betrays our simplistic preoccupation with the flamboyantly spectacular. Think for a moment. A peak is a high point in time, space, or thought, something exciting to achieve but difficult to maintain over time. What we should be seeking is not peak performance but sustained high performance. Instead, blinded by past glories and jaded by our own superlatives, we are like the little boy who fell off the cliff while chasing his kite, all because he failed to keep his feet on the ground.

Getting back on track, building a record of sustained performance, requires a more fundamental shift in theory and practice than many businesses have been willing to make. In their sudden quest for excellence, many firms are making serious mistakes, copying rather than innovating, injecting radical changes into often resistant cultures, and treating performer and environment as separate entities. There is a rush for the new and exciting simply because others are doing it, and a call for ethics and people management because they "add to the bottom line." Many of these innovations are superficial in character and have been applied only in limited areas within the company and with too little concern for their potential ramifications. In all too many cases, American companies have applied band-aids or wielded meat axes where surgery has been needed.

Our quest for simplistic solutions gets us into trouble again and again. We pull managers out of the line, expose them to new ideas, and then toss them back into an unchanged and resistant work environment. Yet we know it won't work. If we take managers out of impossible situations to inspire, motivate, and train, and then return them to the same situations, chances are they'll revert to their old ways in a very short time.

We need an approach and terminology that encompasses both the individual and the environment in a more inclusive way; we need concepts that recognize the kind of manager required and the workplace he or she needs in order to succeed. What is needed is a fundamental reappraisal of the ways we traditionally think about managers and their organizations, a renewed emphasis on basic skills, and a range of approaches designed to bring about a greater coincidence between individual and organizational values and goals.

We've chosen the term "tough/nice" to describe the manager and environment required. Throughout most of this book, we'll be focusing on managers, the men and women who have the power to change the work environment. While our emphasis will be on the people side of management, we'll be engaged in what the Japanese call "nibbling away at the edges" and subtly (we hope) hinting at needed changes in culture, structure, and process.

We've grouped the chapters under four headings: QUALITIES, SKILLS, TASKS, and OVERVIEW. We begin with a rather intensive look at tough/nice managers in terms of five key inner qualities that make them what they are. Then, in chapters 2 through 4, we discuss three skills that are fundamental to tough/nice managers: awareness, communication, and problem solving. These skills are crucial to performing the TASKS described in chapters 5 through 18. Then, in the final chapter, we deal with the challenges of becoming a tough/nice manager.

The basic point to remember is that, in the long run, manager and environment are inextricably linked. The environment must support the manager, and vice versa. People and organizations function better when there is a healthy degree of mutual respect between them.

We have included some questions, or what we call "thought provokers," at the end of each skill and task chapter. Your answers to these questions will enable you to compare your views and operating practices against those of tough/nice managers. And we haven't included a list of "right" answers. These you'll discover for yourself. You may want to look over these questions before you read each chapter, check on your views after having read the chapter or, as one of our readers chose to do, use them as tests, before and after reading each chapter.

This book is meant to be used, read, studied, and practiced. It will work for you only if you apply it. We've tried to keep the chapters short and the language crisp. So, in the interests of conciseness, we'll say no more and let you get on with it.

Shale and Candace Paul

Chapter 1

QUALITIES OF THE TOUGH/NICE MANAGER

Qualities define managers--who they are, how they function, and what they can achieve. Over the long-term, qualities more than anything else determine success.

Qualities of the Tough/Nice Manager

Managers are supposed to be tough-minded. Dedication and drive mark the best of them. Those who rise to the top are bold, aggressive, daring, and sometimes ruthless.

Until recently, those stereotypes had a ring of truth. They fit the concept of the corporation as rigidly hierarchical and controlled. Within the past two decades, however, our perceptions of organizations and managers have shifted significantly. The world has changed, and with it the requirements for survival and success. National economics are becoming increasingly interdependent and subject to rapid, often cataclysmic changes. Few companies are immune. Many are being forced to respond more quickly and imaginatively to growing uncertainties. Managers are having to reappraise their attitudes and approaches, develop new skills, and look more deeply into the inner motivations that can cause them to succeed or fail.

A new breed of managers is emerging. Unlike their predecessors, they grew up in the relative prosperity of recent years. They are at home with changing technology and exploding information. They are concerned with quality, excellence, and caring in their life and work.

4

They are more likely to be found in the smaller, fast-growth companies than in the huge behemoths of the Fortune 500. Their motivations are complex, and they are often impatient with old ways. They are still in the minority and to some extent they are an anomaly, a blend of opposites. They are bold and cautious, decisive and deliberate, tough and nice. They balance intuition and logic in a refreshingly new way of perceiving and deciding.

We've chosen the term "tough/nice" to describe this new breed. As we said, they are emerging, sometimes hard to spot and difficult to understand, for they differ radically from their predecessors. They are more complex, and they view themselves and their jobs quite differently. They can perhaps best be described in terms of five inner qualities that make them what they are.

Inner-Directedness

W e are all influenced by the world around us. We make decisions and take action depending on how we perceive and judge our external environment. Our perception and judgment are altered by internal factors that work in subtle ways. We are inner-directed to the extent that we rely on these factors. At one extreme, we may be totally unmoved by external events; at the other, we are controlled by them.

> *creating an environment which allows our people to function at their full potential.*
>
> **Larry Kendall** - his role as president of The Group, Inc.

Tough/nice managers are highly inner-directed. They often seem unmoved by threatening situations and conflicting views. They draw upon hidden inner resources for solutions that, to their colleagues, often appear unwarranted by the facts. This quality of inner-directedness is a product of six factors, each carefully nurtured and developed.

1. **Stillness**. They have an inner calm that rarely deserts them. They seldom lose their cool and when they do, they seem able to withdraw, regroup, and return unscathed-- recharged and confident. They know they can't think clearly if their minds are filled with noise and trivia, so they consciously empty their minds of all that disturbs

or distracts them from the task at hand. In so doing, they become inwardly attentive. They develop an intuitive grasp of things. Perhaps "develop" isn't the right word. They allow their intuitive capacities to emerge. Stillness, for the tough/nice manager, is a means of getting ego out of the way in order to hear more clearly.

It would be a mistake to conclude that stillness occurs without effort. In fact, it's a product of awareness and self-discipline. Tough/nice managers recognize a need to purposefully distance themselves from the chaos and confusion that attend many problem situations. They have learned through experience that if they allow themselves to become part of the problem, they run a serious risk of losing their objectivity altogether.

2. **Identity and purpose**. Tough/nice managers know who they are and what they are about. They don't think of themselves only as manager, spouse, or parent. Their self-concept involves a wholeness and richness that touch all aspects of their lives.

Identity is essential to purpose. If you don't know who you are and what you have to offer, you'll have a difficult time deciding what you want to achieve. Tough/nice managers begin with the "who" in order to define the "what." They understand that both completeness and uniqueness are within themselves. They are goal-oriented, but in a very special way. They feel things that are important to them. They actual-

> *Identity is essential to purpose. If you don't know who you are and what you have to offer, you'll have a difficult time deciding what you want to achieve.*

ly visualize what it's like to have attained their goals. Their vision inspires and empowers them, shines through to others, and sets them apart from those who are less clear about themselves and their lives. They see connections among all the things in which they are involved. Work, play, family, and rest are part of this interwoven fabric. And not surprisingly, this inclusive sense of purpose invades and molds their attitudes as managers.

Larry Kendall exemplifies this unity of personal and professional purpose. His company, The Group, Inc., a real estate firm located in

Ft. Collins, Colorado offers an unusual approach to entrepreneurship and management. Every permanent full-time employee owns a piece of the firm. Survival means being self-motivated and self-directed. Commitment is high and the results prove it. The firm has been first in sales in Ft. Collins for the past decade. Current sales exceed those of the next four firms combined.

Larry sees his own and his firm's purposes as nearly identical: *"to be the best at what I (we) do."* As president, his role lies in *"creating an environment which allows our people to function at their full potential."* This penchant for being the best seems ingrained in everyone. Words like alignment, vision, values, and mastery are in common usage among the firm's fifty-three members. Enthusiasm and vitality emote from Larry's office all the way to the front desk where Debbie Jones, part owner and receptionist, handles up to 600 calls and contacts per day.

Larry's knack for uniting vision and purpose was evident in the founding of the firm. When he and the original ten partners met eleven years ago, they asked themselves two questions: *"How will real estate be sold in the year 2000?"* and *"How can we do it now?"* They then proceeded to design the firm along approaches suggested by the answers they developed. Larry offers a short piece of advice, stemming undoubtedly from these early perceptions: "Act as if ...". If you want to be something or someone, act as if you already are. Present-focused action, Larry has found, is empowering.

This ability to combine vision and purpose is a predominant characteristic of tough/nice managers. They seem to be able to unite individual and organizational commitment in very personal ways.

3. **A strong sense of values**. Many people have strong values, inherited or borrowed from parents, church, society, and occasional mentors. The values of tough/nice managers are peculiarly their own, and they realize that their values are not necessarily right for others. As a result, they seldom try to convert others to their point of view. Their values are more evident in actions than words. They teach by the example they set and the questions they raise.

Along with others, tough/nice managers have borrowed and inherited some of their truths, but there's a difference. They test them in relation to their own sense of rightness and adapt or discard as appropriate. This testing process is largely internal. They are attentive to outer experience but maintain a detachment that allows them to sort, judge, and decide based on a strong inner centeredness. The frustrating part to many around them is that tough/nice managers feel no compulsion to explain or justify.

Tough/nice managers align themselves with organizations in which they perceive an existing compatibility of values or in which they sense there are opportunities for alignment. It is this quiet inner demand that makes them effective agents of change and leadership for innovative organizations. For those organizations mired in tradition and committed to avoiding change, tough/nice managers pose a threat. And therein lies a key to locating them. They are seldom found in sleepy, sloppy firms dedicated to preserving the status quo. They are where the action is, articulating the vision, stimulating those around them, and helping to bring about that sense of alignment so essential to success.

Tough/nice managers champion the coincident values of their organization and themselves, often in rather simple ways. *"100 percent full on"* are popular words in The Group. *"We do our best all the time"* is another slogan, the simplicity of which belies its effectiveness as a unifying and motivating force. In a sense, it's this combination of personal alignment and ability to articulate that sets tough/nice managers apart from others who are unable to focus their energies in one direction. They are high performers; their aim is better and they consistently achieve more than their peers.

4. **A standard of appropriateness**. Tough/nice managers judge a situation on its merits. They refuse to impose their values on others or to require that others accept their word on faith alone. They sense what works in a given instance because of their keen awareness of the personalities and factors involved. Their standard of appropriateness includes a recognition that their values may not work with others. Their approach is practical--to discover what will work in a given situation, based on an appreciation of the other person's attitudes,

values, and position. They are solution-oriented rather than problem-bound.

5. **High self-esteem**. Tough/nice managers love and respect themselves, accept responsibility for their own lives, and refuse to blame others for things that happen to them. They are active rather than reactive and know that, no matter how bad things seem, there are always options.

Do they get depressed? Do they doubt? Are they ever afraid? Yes, they recognize these emotions as normal reactions to difficult problems and stressful situations. But they don't take them personally. Their high sense of self-esteem enables them to deal objectively with their emotions. They examine their fears and doubts and combat depression in positive, healthful ways. They refuse to allow themselves to become captured by situations.

6. **Confident awareness of a higher order**. They are attentive to the order of things. Like the physicist and theologian, they sense a higher order and intelligence at work. This knowing is intuitive rather than logical, often not empirically provable, but valid nonetheless. This awareness permits them to transcend their personal concerns and gain a larger view. It inspires curiosity, confidence, optimism, and a sense of humor. It instills a view of life events as opportunities rather than problems.

Dynamic Balance

Life is a juggling act. We are constantly pressured to balance work and family, income and security, comfort and challenge. We are confronted with conflicting demands on our time, energies, and resources. It's often hard to reconcile personal values and workplace realities. Just meeting current demands can leave little time or energy for introspection. When we do find time for ourselves, we are often plagued by unresolved issues, unsure what kind of person or manager we should be, and unable to find a place that feels right. We live our lives slightly off balance much of the time. The tragic thing about all this is that those whom this description fits best are the ones most likely to deny it.

We described tough/nice managers as a blend of opposites. This blending gives them something that others lack. What have they discovered that many of us overlook? Very simply, they understand the importance of balance in life. Let's look at what they know.

They understand that there are different kinds of balance. There's the balancing of externals--family and friends, work and play. Then there's the internal process by which they accommodate and balance opposite qualities. Tough/nice managers have both--an ability to harmonize competing demands upon their time and energies and a capacity to incorporate apparently conflicting attitudes and emotions. They can be tough and demanding when the situation requires, and they can also be gentle and compliant. A sense of appropriateness, rather than ego, determines how they respond in any given situation.

Internal balance can be either static or dynamic. Think of it this way. A set of counterweight scales such as a pharmacist uses illustrates static balance--a delicate and fragile stability. The more sensitive the scales, the more easily their balance is disturbed. Some people maintain this kind of precarious balance in their lives. They function reasonably well when things are going as planned,

> *Stability is assured not by standing still, but by constantly moving, learning, adapting, and growing*

but when problems arise, they are easily disturbed and regain their equilibrium only through heroic efforts.

Dynamic balance, on the other hand, is stability in motion. A navigational gyro illustrates this form of balance. It is stable only when it is moving. The moment it stops spinning, it ceases to function. Dynamic balance in life works somewhat the same way. Stability is assured not by standing still, but by constantly moving, learning, adapting, and growing.

Tough/nice managers are dynamically balanced. They adapt quickly to difficult situations and are comfortable, even invigorated, by change. They seldom allow themselves to get stuck in a situation or left without options. How do they do it? Return to the analogy of the gyro for a moment. It is stable because it is "centered," that is, because it spins about its own axis or center. Tough/nice managers are centered as well. Their center is not so much in their heads as in their guts. They have a mix of logical and intuitive, a felt sense that enables them to adapt quickly and easily.

Flexibility

Flexibility is the capacity to adapt. Some view it as weakness, others as strength. The tough, bare-knuckled managers so common in the past yield only when overwhelmed. Their speech is peppered with words like "battle," "terrain," and "tactics"--vestiges of earlier training when management was all command and control. They stand their ground and give way only grudgingly. They are tough, but not nice.

Tough/nice managers hold an entirely different view. Their attitudes result from their own inner-directedness and balance. They can afford to be flexible because they are not afraid to lose. They know who they are and where they are going. They are centered. They view adaptiveness as strength rather than weakness. It is this inner flexibility that enables them to see the other person's viewpoint, explore a wider range of alternatives, and come up with constructive, mutually acceptable solutions.

Viewed in this manner, it is apparent that flexibility is strength. Managers who fear for their jobs or are unsure of their ability get stuck frequently. They cling fiercely to their own point of view and yield only reluctantly. For this kind of manager, life is a constant hassle and combativeness is a way of life.

You can't will yourself to become flexible. Flexibility is a by-product of being centered[1], inner-directed, and balanced. Managers who give up trying to force things and discover the fit and flow of their own lives become powerful, but their power is uniquely their own.

---

[1]In the event that the concept of centering is unfamiliar, the reader may want to refer to an earlier work, The Warrior Within, by Shale Paul, Delta Group Press, Evergreen, Colorado, 1983.

Personal Power

Many managers become intrigued by power. Promises of pay, promotion, and prestige encourage them to view power largely in external terms. They are subtley coached to equate it with titles, compensation, and office decor. Seldom are they encouraged to develop power within themselves, for personally based power threatens all but the best organizations. But if an organization really wants to be the best, it would do well to have its people develop their own sense of power rather than having them become dependent upon externals.

Sooner or later, most managers find the enticements of power wanting. The pay isn't good enough, the job isn't what they expected, or the promised futures are not realized. It is this uncertainty that causes many to doubt themselves and question their goals.

Tough/nice managers understand power. While they recognize its external enticements, they know that those enticements can be illusive and unreal. They seek a deeper source. They see themselves as the center from which their power flows outwardly to others in a gentle, confident way. And those around them gravitate to tough/nice managers as though they know that something important is happening there.

One factor that empowers tough/nice managers is their loyalty, but there's a catch. They are loyal first to themselves, and then to others and to the organization. They recognize that in order to give loyalty to others they must first be loyal to themselves. This inner-based loyalty can be a threat to those higher in the organization. When people recognize that they cannot demand another's loyalty, they often become wary. That's what frequently happens, for tough/nice managers operate from a base of internal strength and are not easily intimidated. They stand up for what they believe, even if it means that they and the organization must part company.

Commitment

No individual, team, or organization can succeed without commitment. Commitment is focus, directing power to achieve an objective. Without commitment, power is dissipated and ineffective.

Coaches and bosses share the burden of inspiring commitment in others. They must find ways to interest, motivate, and challenge their charges to greater heights and deeds.

Tough/nice managers are self-inspired. They commit to an undertaking not so much because the boss says they should, but because they know that strong commitment is essential to their own growth and success. In this perception lies the key to motivating them. Their commitment cannot be demanded; it must be recognized and nurtured. And the secret of nurturing lies in the extent to which tough/nice managers perceive a coincidence between their own and their organization's goals. If they see those goals as complementary, their energy and enthusiasm are unbounded. If on the other hand they sense those goals are at odds and becoming more so, they may leave for greener pastures.

*****

Inner-directedness, balance, flexibility, power, and commitment are the qualities that define the tough/nice manager. Are they genetic gifts given to only a select few, or are they available to us all? At his point, we have only tentative answers. Excellent organizations and high achieving managers are popular topics. We know that certain people possess qualities not shared by others, but we don't know why. We aren't sure how much is due to heredity, environment, or just plain hard work. But we have discovered two things.

First, individuals can learn to be more inner-directed. Moreover, it appears that this learning is more a product of discovery than development, that it consists of finding what is really true about oneself rather than struggling to become something one is not. The former is a function of awareness, the latter of manipulation.

Second, organizations can provide conditions that make such discoveries more likely--where individual excellence and difference are respected, where both individual and organizational goals are important, and where decisions are made in ways that inspire commitment rather than resistance.

Excellence in individuals and organizations is still the exception rather than the rule. Excellent organizations such as Dana Corporation, Hewlett-Packard, Honda, and McDonalds are still in the minority. Mediocrity is more common, especially in large organizations. The tough/nice manager represents a model of excellence and a goal for organizations that want to develop excellent managers.

For the man or woman who aspires to be exceptional, these five qualities--inner-directedness, dynamic balance, flexibility, personal power, and commitment--represent conditions under which spectacular performance is most likely to occur. The trick is to find ways to encourage their emergence in one's own experience. The process involves a mastery of certain fundamental skills, the development of some equally fundamental attitudes, and the practice of specific approaches to the management tasks at hand.

Chapter 2

BUILDING AWARENESS

Why is it that some people are automatically more aware than others? Is it because they have a higher degree of intelligence or because they work at being aware?

Building Awareness

Ray Ashton is a management consultant with a large national consulting firm. He specializes in helping troubled organizations regain organizational health. Occasionally he completes an assignment in a few days. More often, he spends several weeks with the client, interviewing, gathering information, and testing conclusions. Ray tells of an incident that affected his entire approach to consulting:

When I first became a consultant, I was assigned to work with a senior partner in the firm, a stiff rather humorless man named John who had a penchant for exactness. We were involved in an organization study for a client in upper New York state. Our task was to study the headquarters and field staffs with an eye to making the organization more effective.

The first day we met with the chairman, the president, and several key managers. As we left our last interview late in the afternoon, I asked John if he had plans for dinner. "Yes," he replied, "I have to draft the final report." "Are you working on another study?" I asked. "No, this one," he countered. I was incredulous. We were one day and half a dozen interviews into the study and he was writing the final report! John watched as mixed emotions crossed my face, the slightest hint of a smile playing about his lips, and then continued: "Consulting, good consulting, is at least 50 percent intuition. It's the feel you get for things, a sense that something's not right or that there's something missing. With experience, you learn to detect signs early. I test my intuition, my early warnings, constantly. I do it by writing the final report as early as possible, often after only a day with the client. Invariably, I find that these early impressions are invaluable when it comes to sorting through the mountains of information we consultants gather.

In later years and other situations, I learned to apply this early lesson. I found that intuition, based on experience, can make a difference. Knowing when to go with your gut and not be misled by sometimes overwhelming evidence to the contrary is often the difference between mediocre and outstanding results.

*****

Price Cobb had just come out of a turn into a long straightaway in the 1987 LeMans race. The course was slick and oily. His speed was approaching 180 miles an hour when suddenly his car began to slide sideways, became airborne, and crashed. The car disintegrated; fuel from a ruptured tank streamed into the cockpit and ignited. Price talked about it afterwards:

> This wasn't my first crash, but it was the worst. The car was completely destroyed and most of my fireproof clothing was burned off. You know, these things happen in a few seconds at most. One moment you're roaring down the track at 180 and the next moment everything's falling apart. When the fuel began spewing all over my lap, I knew I was in trouble. It all happened so fast, there wasn't really time to take any action, even if I could have figured how to get out of it. The point is, the moment that the fuel caught fire, the entire scene went into slow motion. It was as though I was watching everything as a casual observer with all the time in the world. I wasn't afraid, nor was there any feeling of pain, only a detached interest in what was happening. And you know, I walked away from that one without a scratch.

*****

What has all this to do with management, and particularly with the tough/nice manager? Very simply, those who excel--consultants, race car drivers, athletes, and managers--develop special capacities for high awareness. Their awareness is not that of the average man or woman. Ray Ashton learned that intuitive awareness can often outweigh the obvious facts and so lead to important conclusions. Price Cobb experienced a reorienting of time so significant that it altered his entire perceptions of the event. In every profession, outstanding performance and high awareness are linked.

Awareness is especially critical to Gerry Leary, an auto mechanic who owns his own business in Boulder, Colorado. As he puts it, *"Awareness is the biggest insurance policy I have. It doesn't cost anything in money, but it is the most difficult to maintain."* Operating in an industry where ethics are often sadly lacking, Gerry is somewhat unique. He has established a solid reputation for being fair and honest with his clients, "friends" as he calls them. He reports that, while the majority of his clients are honest, some perhaps reacting to the industry's reputation, are not. Gerry relies upon his keen awareness of voice sounds to help him gauge their honesty. You might think that he is overly sensitive on the subject, but you see, Gerry has been blind since birth. His life and livelihood depend, to a much greater degree than most of us, on awareness. Talk with him for only a few minutes, and you will be impressed, not only with how much he perceives, but with how much he knows. At age 35, he is a wealth of unusual perspectives about life. In a sense, he "sees" more than many of us who have the full use of all of our senses.

Tough/nice managers, too, have developed their own special forms of awareness. They approach life with interest, curiosity, humor, and detachment. They observe, question, and listen. They have high sensory receptivity--an ability to use all five senses to develop information. Finally, they are attentive to the subtle continuous mind/body dialogue we call intuition. This sixth sense enables them to process information differently and allows them to be comfortable "going with the gut."

Awareness is first a function of intent. You must want to be aware in order to let go of the preconceptions and prejudices that block awareness. A desire to know and a willingness to face facts increases awareness. In Gerry Leary's case, the decision was obvious. He had to fine-tune all of his available senses in order to realize full awareness. How open are you? How badly do you want to learn? How willing are you to look objectively at problems, even at the risk of having to give up favorite assumptions and safe positions?

It's often difficult to change intent. Fear, anger, defensiveness, ignorance, and insecurity tempt us to resist becoming fully aware. Opinion and bias are often more comfortable than fact and objectivity. Still, changing intent is a matter of decision. Once you decide to become more aware, the task becomes much easier.

Awareness is also a function of attention. Poor attention skills can cause you to make mistakes. As a manager, you're paid to notice small things--an overlooked fact, a veiled threat, or a slight shift in emotional climate. Ray Ashton's habit of early final report writing vastly improved his attentional skills.

Tough/nice managers know that in many situations, it's the small things that count. They train themselves and their employees to be attentive.

There are many ways to increase your awareness. They range from subtle changes in eye patterns to fundamental shifts in your attitudes toward others. Here are some you might want to try.

1. Learn to avoid filtering and prejudging. Your beliefs, prejudices, and history can cause you to filter information that comes to you. Face it, as a manager you have strong opinions about many things. You've achieved a level of success by acting in certain ways. So it's often difficult to act contrary to your own views, because they've worked for you in the past. But how can you be sure your prejudices are justified or your opinions based on fact?

A simple way is to develop the practice of testing your conclusions frequently. When you are tempted to make a strong conclusive statement about a situation or a person, ask yourself:

- Do I <u>know</u> this to be fact?
- Am I <u>assuming</u> it to be fact?
- How can I determine which it is?
- What if it <u>is</u> so?
- What if it <u>isn't</u>?

Asking these questions repeatedly will cause you to become more aware, less opinionated, and more open to new ideas. At the same time, you want to be attentive to the source of your feelings about things and people. Often your intuition will tell you things that "facts" won't. Be alert to your intuitive side. We'll be talking more about that in just a moment.

2. Develop a questioning attitude. Your key to success as a manager lies not in giving information but in getting it. Tough/nice managers know how to listen and how to focus outside themselves on the person or subject. Their interest and concern are reflected in the questions they ask. They know that properly phrased questions can build trust and rapport, establish control, help others to solve their own problems, and encourage greater openness.

Major behavioral changes often begin with subtle shifts in attitude. Simply deciding to ask more questions can cause you to become more curious. Making a habit of asking questions is a form of operant conditioning--the act of repeated questioning gradually causes you to <u>want</u> to know more. Knowing becomes contagious. If you learn to approach situations from the standpoint of what you don't know, you'll discover that something can be gained from every encounter. You'll find also that others are attracted to you because they sense your interest and concern. It all begins with a questioning attitude. Asking conveys openness; telling reveals a closed mind.

3. Become a skilled questioner. Asking questions is an art. Tough/nice managers gain tremendous amounts of information and are able to control the conversation simply by the questions they ask.

You can't ask intelligent questions unless you know what you want to find out. So begin by making a list of what you need to know, and then formulate your questions. Be aware that there are five different types of questions, each designed for a specific purpose:

Open ended. Typically, an open-ended question begins with *"how"* or *"what"* and can't be answered with a simple yes or no. It requires the other person to expand upon his or her answer. For example, consider the question, "How do you explain employee attitudes since the recent pay raise?" In this case, a yes or no answer won't suffice.

Close ended. A close-ended question can be answered with a simple yes or no. Since a *"no"* answer can stop a conversation, close-ended questions must be used carefully and posed in positive terms where possible. For example, the question, *"Do you see how you could benefit by participating more in the meetings?"* encourages an affirmative response.

Clarifying. A clarifying question is designed to get the other person to expand on or explain what he or she has just said. It can also help to defuse a tense situation. What if, for example, an employee bursts into your office and says, *"I can't take it anymore. I'm going to quit."* You might respond, *"That sounds very distressing. Can you tell me what's wrong?"*

Leading. A leading question is intended to move the other person in a specific direction and to encourage agreement. Leading questions are often preceded by a short statement that establishes control. For example: "You said you felt you could complete the project by the end of the month, isn't that true?"

Assumptive. Assumptive questions are used to gain agreement, confirm your understanding, and surface underlying disagreements. They are always based on an implicit assumption. The question, *"Which day is better for you to make up your work, Tuesday or Wednesday?"* assumes that the person has already agreed to make up the work.

It's important that you know how to use these different question types. Each has a specific purpose. You should, however, avoid preplanning an entire meeting by designing all of your questions beforehand. Remember, the key to awareness is listening. If you are so preoccupied with the next question, you may miss what is being said. Determine the facts you need to know, plan your first couple of questions, and then let the conversation take its own course. Frequently, you'll find that each answer evokes another question.

Another technique for becoming a skilled questioner is simply to respond to a question with a question. This is especially useful when the subject matter is complex or when tensions are high. A question requires a pause and encourages the other person to think further before replying. Moreover, your question lets the other know that you are interested in finding out what was meant by the original question. By way of example, an initial question might be: *"Can't you see that I'm really upset by what happened today?"* Your answer, a second question, might be: "Would you mind sharing your feelings with me so that I can be more helpful?"

4. Improve your attention skills. Tough/nice managers practice their attention skills constantly. They know that high awareness, like physical fitness, requires regular exercise. Both awareness and the body decline quickly from lack of use. The secret is to develop conscious habits that will encourage heightened awareness. Here are some you can use.

Look for exceptions. Learn to notice things that are different, unusual, or unexpected--an object out of place in your office or a sentence in a report that doesn't seem to fit. We fail to notice countless things in our lives simply because we are not alert.

Listen for names. If you forget someone's name immediately after you've been introduced, chances are you weren't paying attention. Listen carefully. If you aren't sure of the name, ask the person to repeat or spell it. People are flattered when you care enough to get it right. Repeat the name silently two or three times, and notice how it sounds in your mind. If you have a problem remembering certain people's names, find a rhyming word or visual image to associate with the name and the person. If you've met several people at a meeting or a party, take a few minutes when you're driving back to your home or office to remember them. Repeat their names and visualize their faces and the circumstances under which you were introduced. If you noticed something significant about another person, or if you discovered a mutual interest, recall it. You'll be surprised how much these simple devices will help you remember.

Let questioning become a habit. When you're introduced to someone, how often do you search frantically for something to say? Instead of telling the other person something about yourself, ask a question. Make it a point to find out at least one fact about everyone you meet. Once you start it's easy, and it makes it easier to remember that person later. It also lets people know that you are interested in them.

Practice soft focus. Most people develop set patterns of observing people and things around them. For example, if you're threading a needle or fitting two small parts together, you may squint and furrow your eyebrows in order to see more clearly. Some people do the same thing when introduced to someone else, as though they're trying to see every wrinkle in the other person's face. This is called "hard focus," and while there are many variations, it usually involves a certain physical tenseness in the eyes and face, in fact, throughout the entire body. But there's a more important connection--the relationship between the kind of focus you use and the part of the brain it accesses. Hard focus addresses the left, or logical, side of the brain. If you are analyzing things logically, you are probably using hard focus.

Soft focus, on the other hand, involves a more relaxed use of the eyes. With soft focus, you take in a broader field of vision rather than a single point, and you access the right, intuitive side of the brain. Most of us rely too much on hard focus, with the result that we curb our intuitive perceptions. Pros like Price Cobb learn to go into a soft-focus state even in life-threatening situations. Why? That subtle mind/body link on which they rely tells them it's an effective way to deal with crisis. The altered states they achieve afford a level of objectivity and calm unattainable any other way.

Interviewing provides an excellent example of the advantages of using both hard and soft focus. The next time you interview someone, make it a point to avert your eyes from them for a few moments. Let your eyes gently rest on some distant object, perhaps a tree outside, so that you see the person only with your peripheral vision. Then listen to what they're saying. Note how you feel about them and their words. Do you get a sense that they are sincere? Confident? Uncomfortable? You'll be surprised how much you can pick up by this simple device.

Learn passive attention. This is a broader form of soft focus, what is sometimes termed an "alpha/theta state" in meditation. It's a way of perceiving that incorporates both intuition (feelings) and logic (thoughts) simultaneously. It requires practice, but it's actually fairly easy. Here's how to do it.

Sit in a comfortable chair with your hands folded. Lower you head slightly and close your eyes. Take a deep breath and hold it for about a minute, allow the air to sink down into the lower abdomen as you relax. Now exhale gradually through the mouth in a long, slow exhalation. Continue breathing naturally with your eyes closed, only make it a point to exhale in this way each time--make it long, slow, and through the mouth. After a few exhalations, you'll notice that it takes longer and longer for you to exhale, perhaps as long as thirty seconds. This indicates deeper relaxation. Continue breathing in this manner and observe how your body feels. Your limbs become heavy, and you may notice a sense of warmth in your body--and you'll feel very relaxed. Now let your mind turn gently to some problem you've been working on. Don't try to solve it; just allow it to appear in your consciousness and observe what happens. Do you feel differently about the problem now? Are you aware of additional apparently un-related ideas that seem to be connecting themselves with the problem? If so, notice them, make it a point to remember them, but don't judge them.

This entire process will take no more than ten minutes. After a while, you'll sense that you have a better grasp of the problem and that you are ready to move on. When this happens, open your eyes slowly and don't focus on any one object. Remain seated and review what has happened. You may be surprised at the additional perspectives you've gathered about the problem. You may, for example, realize that you've discovered a solution you hadn't considered before.

Test your intuition. We all have hunches, feelings about situations or people. We often discount those feelings in favor of assumptions, logic, and facts. When we do, we are suppressing the intuitive side of our awareness.

The next time you have a hunch about a situation, write it down. You may want to keep a small notebook to record your hunches and later check out how accurate they were. If you're not accustomed to trusting your intuition, it might help to know that scientists have discovered that our first impressions are usually the correct ones. Later impressions are more often less accurate. Also, if you're unaccustomed to following your hunches, you may be surprised to find that they are at least partially right much of the time. You may anticipate a future event, but be off by several days. Your precision will improve with practice but your practice must be gentle, almost effortless. Tuning in to the intuition is a delicate process in which there's no room for will. All you need to do is to allow your intuitive to work!

*****

Awareness, rather than intelligence, is the first stepping stone to success. It fact, intelligence may inhibit awareness because intellect alone too often relies exclusively on logic and hard, narrow focus.

Thought Provokers

1. _____ Are you aware of the extent to which your beliefs and prejudices control your judgments, decisions, and actions?

2. _____ Do you often find that these biases, rather than objective determination,
control your actions?

3. _____ Do you consider yourself to be open and willing to face facts and look at problems objectively?

4. _____ Do others react to you in ways that confirm your openness?

5. _____ Do you feel that you are confronted with an inordinate number of problems?

6. _____ Do you feel that these problems prevent you from being fully effective as a manager?

7. _____ As you think of mistakes you've made, did most of them result from a lack of awareness on your part?

8. _____ Do you typically approach situations on the basis of what you know rather than what you need to know?

9. _____ Do you understand the differences between various types of questions (e.g., assumptive, open-ended, clarifying)?

10. _____ Do you take time to figure out what you need to know before asking questions?

11. _____ When confronted with a need to gather information from others, do you preplan your questions?

12. _____ In conflict situations, do you more often find yourself arguing your point of view rather than asking questions?

13. _____ As a manager, do you find it more useful to instruct others than to encourage them by asking leading questions?

14. _____ Do you typically think of communication as a continuing opportunity for increasing your own awareness?

15. _____ When introduced to someone, do often find yourself telling rather than asking?

16. _____ Do you maintain frequent eye contact when talking with another person?

17. _____ Do you regard yourself primarily as a logical person?

18. _____ Are you aware of when you are using hard and soft focus styles?

19.____ Do you regularly use passive attention as a means of increasing your awareness?

20.____ Are you confident in the accuracy of your impressions of people and situations?

Chapter 3

COMMUNICATING EFFECTIVELY

Poor communicators make poor managers. The problem is that many people <u>think</u> they relate well to others when, in actuality, they do not.

Communicating Effectively

Graduates of Cornell University's 1953 and 1954 MBA classes will remember Ed Litchfield. As dean of the Graduate School of Business & Public Administration during those years, he was also chairman of the board of Smith Corona Marchant and soon was to become chancellor of the University of Pittsburgh. Dr. Litchfield was renowned for his ability as a speaker and moderator. He could listen to half a dozen speeches and then, with scarcely a note, take the floor and synthesize them all in his concluding remarks. He had an even more remarkable talent. As a college dean, chief executive, and soon-to-be chancellor, Ed Litchfield's schedule was beyond full.

> *Communication involves awareness, tact, and caring. It entails the accomodation of different attitudes, objectives, and personalities. Often, it involves conflict.*

Still, he had time for his students. Whether you had ten minutes or an hour with him, you left convinced that during that time you had his complete attention. Even the most lowly graduate student left his office feeling valued.

Communication involves awareness, tact, and caring. It entails the accommodation of different attitudes, objectives, and personalities. Often, it involves conflict.

Managers are supposed to be good communicators, even though most have had little formal communications training. Somehow, it is assumed that they are skilled because they are constantly involved with people. The fact is, many managers do <u>not</u> communicate well. Instead they rely on technical expertise, authority, or a particular style to carry them through.

Tough/nice managers know that their success depends on their ability to communicate with those above, below, and beside them. They realize that effective communication requires high awareness and constant practice. They work at being effective communicators. They are alert to the pitfalls and strive to overcome them.

Pitfalls to Effective Communication

Six factors account for most failures in communication:

1. **Conflicting Objectives.** We often assume that our objectives are compatible with those of others. If we have something to say, we assume everyone else wants to hear it. If we have a goal in mind, we assume others share it. If we give instructions, we expect others to obey willingly. In many instances, our assumptions are incorrect.

2. **Lack of Clarity.** Clarity is a shared responsibility. Both sender and receiver have an implicit obligation to ensure that a common understanding exists. All too often, two people hear the same words but interpret them differently due to disparities in awareness, education, or experience.

3. **Loaded words or threats**. We all learn quickly how to *"get"* the other person by using irritating words or phrases. When we do, we provoke reactions that frustrate effective communication.

4. **Filtering**. Few people accept information without modifying it. Personal history, values, prejudice, and fear cause us to tailor what we hear to fit our way of thinking. When we do, we lose the original

meaning. Often, our filters are applied at the subconscious level and we're not even aware of them. What you meant and what I thought you meant are often miles apart.

5. **Hidden agendas**. People don't always say what they mean. Fear of the reaction and a reluctance to confront issues directly encourage hidden agendas--unspoken attempts to direct the conversation and influence the outcome in subtle ways.

6. **Insensitivity to non-verbal messages**. Some authorities contend that as much as 75 percent of our communication is unspoken. Non-verbal and verbal messages often conflict. The verbal component reflects the speaker's conscious thoughts; the non-verbal component reflects subconscious motivations.

Unless you are aware of these pitfalls and consciously work to overcome them, they can have a negative impact upon every exchange.

Realities of Communication

Tough/nice managers are aware how they relate to others and understand the following basics of the communication process:

1. Communication is a two way street. In order for communication to be effective, a message must be sent, received, and understood. The sender has a responsibility to listen and the receiver a similar responsibility to respond.

2. Communication involves risk. Whenever you share something with another person, there is always the possibility of doubt, disagreement, or challenge.

3. Both parties subconsciously apply their own attitudes and prejudices to the conversation.

4. Much of the time, we don't know if an exchange has been effective. We can be sure only if we are attentive to both verbal and non-verbal aspects, repeatedly ask questions, and listen carefully to the answers.

5. Awareness is an unnatural act. High awareness is a result of conscious intent. To the degree that we become preoccupied with our own concerns, we miss what the other person says.

6. Conflicting objectives exist in both social and work situations. Communication, therefore, is a process of understanding, clarifying, and accommodating so that both parties benefit.

7. Communication failures occur in relation to the complexity of the issues involved and the intensity of the participants' emotions. Fear, anger, and hostility are inimical to clarity.

Steps to More Effective Communication

Becoming an effective communicator takes time and practice. Tough/nice managers strive constantly to improve their communication style. They know that by diligently adhering to certain basic techniques, they _will_ improve. Everyone can improve his or her communication style. Here are some things you can do:

1. **Think before you speak!** Ask yourself: What do I really want to say? How can I say it clearly and concisely? How will what I say impact the other person?

2. **Don't be afraid to ask!** Asking someone to repeat or clarify doesn't mean that you weren't listening. It means that you're interested in what the other person has to say and that you want to be sure you understand.

3. **Use the LAREL formula.** This is a simple way to be sure you've covered all the bases. It consists of five steps:
Listen
Ask
Repeat
Expand
Legitimize
Be sure you heard what was said. Ask, if there is any doubt. Repeat back what you think you heard, perhaps in slightly different words, and ask for confirmation. Then expand on what the other person has said to help ensure that you really do understand. Finally, in the case of a dispute, legitimize (_"I can see why you feel that way"_).

This confirms your understanding without indicating that you necessarily agree.

4. Don't use loaded words or threats. They only antagonize the other person and encourage defensiveness.

5. Accept statements at face value. What someone else says may not be true. A man's words may tell you how he feels or how he wants you to <u>think</u> he feels; chances are, you won't know which it is at the time. In such situations, withholding judgment frees you to tackle the real issues:

- Why did he say that?
- Does he believe it is true?
- Is it true?
- What will happen if it is (or is not) true?

Accepting statements at face value helps prevent misjudgments and encourages objective listening.

6. Learn to recognize and deal with hidden agendas. People with hidden agendas inevitably drop clues--gaps, inconsistencies in logic, *"don't tread on me"* statements, or shifts in eye contact, voice tone, or body language. Once you become aware of a hidden agenda, it's relatively easy to overcome. Three steps are involved:

(a) Use direct clarifying questions to determine that the agenda exists. Ask additional questions, if necessary, to flush out the real agenda.

(b) Encourage the other person to share his or her real concerns. If you are fairly certain what the agenda is, you might want to identify it in the form of another question, e.g., *"Is your real concern that you won't get the promotion you want?"*

(c) Seek solutions. In most situations, there may be several. Ask the other person for solutions or suggest some of your own. You can even agree that the once hidden agenda will be off limits for discussion. In any case, try to get the other person to take responsibility for reaching a mutually acceptable solution.

7. **When you sense fear, anger, or defensiveness in the other person, deal with it.**

8. **Be alert to detect insensitivity, myopia, or prejudice.** Remember, people are often unaware of their own feelings. You do them a favor if you can help them become more aware of how these factors can frustrate effective communication. Even in the case of extreme prejudice, it is essential that both parties recognize its potential destructiveness.

9. **Study your own and others' communication styles, and learn how different styles can be used.** Some people are direct and action oriented, while others approach issues laterally and prefer lengthy deliberation. Some feel a need to express themselves fully; others say as little as possible in order to make a point. Each style has advantages and disadvantages. Know the differences and understand how they interact one with another.

Management situations typically afford less flexibility in communications because they are objective oriented. Tough/nice managers are direct in their communications--most of the time-- because they are attentive to the need for decisions and solutions. They keep the exchange on track even at the expense of requiring the other person to change communication style. When the tough/nice manager is indirect or vague, it is by design, to allow the other person to reach his or her own conclusions or to challenge him or her to take action.

10. **Learn how to relate to people on the basis of where they are.** Disparities in education or experience often impose invisible barriers. When people feel inadequate, they are hesitant to share their views or disagree. It is incumbent upon you, the manager, to sense this reluctance and decide what can be done about it. In some instances, the solution is simple -- assuring the other person that his or her views are useful and needed. In other situations, retraining or reassignment may be required.

*****

Successful communicators decide beforehand what results they want and determine what degree of control they must maintain in order to achieve those results.

Thought Provokers

1._____ Are you almost always comfortable communicating with others?

2._____ Do you find it necessary to practice communication skills continually?

3._____ Do you want to hear what you have to say?

4._____ Do you expect your instructions to be followed willingly?

5._____ Do you accept what others say at face value, that is, as expressions of their point of view and not necessarily fact?

6._____ Do you feel that people often don't say what they mean, that frequently there is a hidden non-verbal message?

7._____ Are you aware of the non-verbal aspects of every communication exchange?

8._____ Do you feel obligated to defend yourself when someone challenges you?

9._____ Are you comfortable asking questions even if you are unfamiliar with the subject matter?

10. _____ Do you recognize hidden agendas?

11. _____ Does it bother you having to deal with someone who is fearful or defensive?

12. _____ Do you confront prejudice when you encounter it?

13. _____ Do you understand your own communication style?

14. _____ Do you speak condescendingly when talking to someone who is less educated or less experienced?

15. _____ Do you communicate differently in business and social situations?

16. _____ Do you feel that one person assumes control in most job-related communications?

Chapter 4

PROBLEM SOLVING

Problem solvers are made, not born. Problem solving as a skill relies on awareness, perspective, method, and discipline.

Problem Solving

D ave Bond, a real estate consultant from Washington, D.C., tells of a lesson he learned in problem solving. He had been retained by a large developer to conduct a feasibility study on the development of three land parcels in Chicago's lakeshore district. His client intended to build a large high-rise apartment building on the best of the three sites. Here is Dave's story.

> I spent nearly a month developing information comparing the pros and cons of each parcel. Finally, after several late nights and many long hours, we scheduled the client presentation.
>
> We met in the boardroom--myself, another staff member, the client, and his architect. We presented demographic and site information on each parcel, beginning with the least favorable one. Our intent was to describe the process by which we reached our conclusions and then make our recommendations. As we discussed the first parcel, the client became uneasy. When we moved to the second parcel, his irritation became more apparent. Finally, he leaned forward in his chair and said, "Yes, yes, I know all that. But which piece are you recommending?" I replied we were coming to that, but that we felt it was important that he understand the reasons for our choice. He would have none of it. "I don't care about that," he exclaimed, "I want to know which one you chose." It was clear that he could not be put off any longer. "The first one," I replied. "Thank God," he said, "I bought it yesterday!"

Dave's story reveals a significant insight about problem solvers and problem solving. Dave was quite correctly concerned with the method by which he arrived at his recommendations. His client, on the other hand, was interested only in the result. He had risked

42

thousands of dollars on his conviction as to which was the best parcel.

Effective problem solvers are solution oriented. They quickly identify those few factors that make the difference and arrive intuitively at solutions. In nearly every industry and profession, there are those who are willing to *"go with their gut."* What makes them different?

Tough/nice managers are effective problem solvers. They approach a problem from a specific perspective, apply methods that work for them, and stay with the problem beyond the point of frustration. Their ability to solve problems is partly a function of the qualities we discussed in chapter 1. Let's examine how these qualities affect his approach.

1. **Inner-directedness.** The intuition of tough/nice managers is inspired by their inner-directedness. They first look within and rely on their own resources for solutions. They take responsibility for results. As one intuitive woman executive put it, "If its going to be, it's up to me." In problem solving, there's simply no room for timidity or for the vain hope that someone will bail you out.

For the tough/nice manager, it's a matter of perspective. Problems are challenges, opportunities, tests of one's inner strength. No problem is without a solution; there are always options, alternatives, and possibilities. Tough/nice managers see the world in terms of possibilities--what can happen, what might be true, and what they can do. Reliance on others comes later and only after their own resources have been thoroughly exhausted.

2. **Balance.** The perspective that tough/nice managers have is also a function of their sense of balance--their ability to accommodate opposites within themselves and their life, and their awareness that their strength derives from their centeredness and comfort with change. They are not overly affected by sudden shifts in the problem situation or by the introduction of unexpected variables. They accept the world as it is and move on to solutions.

Their capacity for accommodating opposites makes the tough/nice managers especially effective in reconciling differences and harmonizing discordant factions. They understand that conflict is often a prerequisite for solution.

3. **Flexibility.** Many people become brittle with age. Many managers become inflexible with experience--rigid in their views and defensive of their positions. Inflexibility is usually the result of ig-norance or fear. We don't know enough to realize we're wrong, or we're afraid that yielding may lessen us in the eyes of others.

The opposite is more likely to be true for tough/nice managers. They seek awareness rather than certainty and welcome new ideas. Their constant preoccupation with becoming more fully aware makes them more open. This openness works to their advantage in solving problems. Rather than rejecting an alternative out-of-hand, they are more likely to ask, *"Is there some way it might work?"* They recognize that flexibility in metals and managers is strength rather than weakness. Their often innovative

> *Inflexibility is usually the result of ignorance or fear.*

solutions are, in part, a result of their willingness to look at all the op-tions, however absurd or unpalatable they may at first appear.

4. **Power.** Weak managers cause more problems than they solve. So too do managers who base their power on positions, pay, or pres-tige. Their solutions are marked by *"shoulds"* and *"oughts"* and their management style is marred by a reliance on warnings, threats, and insults.

As we observed earlier, the power of tough/nice managers springs from their inner-directedness and centeredness. They are confident in their ability, always eager to find a better way, and undisturbed when proven wrong. Their power is contagious. It inspires and enables others to adopt an *"I can"* attitude. They train others to be-come better problem solvers, not by what they say but by what they do.

5. **Commitment.** Something less than half of today's managers are fully committed to their work. The rest operate from a base of insecurity, indecision, and lack. Their failure to commit fully stems from the unmet expectations they have imposed upon the world, or from things they perceive have been *"done"* to them. In psychological terms, their locus of control is outer-directed and their energies are dissipated.

Tough/nice managers are a model for those who aspire to do better. For them, the reward is the achievement itself, and every event is significant and instructive. The commitment of tough/nice managers is most evident in the discipline that is an inherent a part of their life. They tackle problems eagerly and pursue solutions enthusiastically.

*****

In this and the two preceding chapters, we've been discussing skills: awareness, communication, and problem solving. Skills are learnable, teachable. Qualities are not. Qualities are innate; they must be discovered rather than developed. The idea that you can develop deep inner qualities violates both neurological and spiritual principles. Researchers in various disciplines have observed the unique nature of holographic reality, which reveals that all the world's knowledge is contained in every single molecule. Thus, according to this theory, all knowledge is already contained in each mind, complete, intact, and waiting to be accessed. This means that we are, if we would only recognize it, in a constant state of completeness. Think of it--you potentially possess all knowledge in a single molecule so small that it is unseen by the naked eye!

Whether you view the holographic concept as metaphor or reality, it does suggest that learning is more a matter of discovery than creation. But what do these ideas have to do with problem solving, you, and the tough/nice manager? How can you apply them in a practical way?

Think of skills both as abilities you can use and as tools for discovering more about yourself. We have long known that some of our most effective learning comes from modeling and repetition. What we're talking about might be called "integrative learning," the melding of concept and application that occurs naturally when we simultaneously employ mind and body in the act of doing.

The steps that follow, as well as those included in the earlier skills chapters, are designed to promote integrative learning. Simply following them will result in changes, discoveries, and increased awareness. In other words, modeling the examples set by the tough/nice manager will encourage you to recognize those qualities within yourself. When this happens, you are no longer blindly following a formula. You are acting from your own internal base of awareness and power. Now, let's turn to the steps of problem solving.

1. **Practice seeing problems as opportunities.** When a problem arises, instead of asking *"Why me?"* or *"Why now?"*, ask *"What can I learn from this experience?"* And don't be dismayed if problems come in pairs or bunches--they do! It may be difficult to realize that seemingly unrelated problems are actually part of a larger learning experience, but often they are.

2. **Remember, problems are seldom as bad as they appear.** It's natural to react when things go wrong, but when you do, you become controlled by the situation. You then lose sight of the fact that there are always options, alternatives, and additional possibilities.

3. **Ask what you can do to solve the problem.** Simply asking implies a willingness to take responsibility for the situation. Adopting an *"I can"* attitude is empowering, and it begins by asking questions. Apply the questioning techniques you learned in the Communications chapter. You'll find that a questioning attitude encourages inner-directedness.

4. **Don't shrink from conflict.** In difficult situations, people often become defensive and angry. Controlled confrontation can clear the air, lessen tensions, and expose hidden agendas.

5. **Avoid predispositioning.** Past experience, if you lean on it excessively, can prevent you from coming up with innovative solutions. We impede our own progress by the assumptions we make, the conditions we impose, and the expectations we hold. You don't want to be part of the problem. One way to avoid it is, at least in the early stages, to accept anything as possible. Brainstorm, ask outlandish questions, and conjure up all manner of *"what ifs."*

6. **Have a system.** You may have your own approach, or you may want to use the consulting formula: DACR/S (Describe, Analyze, Conclude, Recommend/Solve) Whichever you choose, there are some obvious steps you'll want to include:

(a) Define the problem. Be sure you see the whole real problem. Be certain your definition is inclusive and that others agree with your statement.

(b) Begin gathering facts. Notice we said "begin." Fact finding is an ongoing process. Too may managers stop gathering facts when they begin developing conclusions, sometimes with disastrous results. New facts can emerge anytime. Be attentive not to reject them just because they don't seem to fit or because they may undermine some of your earlier efforts.

Look for patterns. Are some things consistent and others random? Do you sense an underlying order in the way things are appearing?

(d) Step back. When you become frustrated, it may be time to get some distance. Sleep on it. Adopt a playful attitude and allow your subconscious mind to work. Your best insights will often come when you're relaxed, unconcerned, and thinking about something else.

(e) Get a feel for the problem. Try some simple relaxation or meditation techniques. Often, when you are in a meditative state, answers come as mentally verbalized words, pictures, or feelings. Be alert for metaphor in these silent inner messages, and occasionally comedy. The universe has a sense of humor and often goes to great lengths to prevent us from taking ourselves too seriously!

(f) Test your intuition. Keep a written record of thoughts that come to you, as a means of testing your insights. You might want to adopt Ray Ashton's habit of *"writing the final report"* early on in the process. Recording and checking your insights helps you develop your intuitive abilities.

(g) Don't discount the absurd. Some thoughts that come may seem unrelated or inappropriate. Don't discard them too quickly; they supply needed prompting to open your thinking to new possibilities.

7. **Set an example by what you do.** As a manager, you're accustomed to having others take their lead from you. Where possible, have them learn by watching you in action rather than hearing you preach. Practice works best. If you act calmly, deliberately, and avoid prejudging, you'll be amazed at the stabilizing effect on others.

8. **Seek permanent, win/win solutions.** In stressful situations, it's natural to accept compromises and band-aid solutions or to opt for the course that meets your needs even though others are dissatisfied. Resist the temptation. Make the extra effort that enables all sides to benefit from the experience.

9. **Understand your own and others' creative styles.** We mentioned the need to step back and get a feel for the problem. We each have different times when we're more creative. We also have different ways of reaching solutions. You may work best by talking it out. Someone else may need to write everything down stream-of-consciousness style. The point is, be respectful of your own and others' styles.

10. **Look for the lesson.** When you've reached a solution and begun taking steps to implement it, there's still one more thing to do. Nearly every problem affords lessons beyond the immediate situation. Take time to discover those lessons. Often you can apply the same techniques used in solving the original problem -- stepping back, looking at the experience in a detached and nonjudgmental way.

*****

Earlier we said that following the steps in these three skill chapters leads back to the essential underlying qualities. Well, the same holds true for the next section, chapters 5 through 18. In each of those chapters, we discuss attitudes and approaches that distinguish the tough/nice manager's performance with respect to a particular task. You can approximate that performance and gain insight into its deeper significance simply by practicing the steps involved.

Thought Provokers

1. _____ Do you see problem solving as part of your job?

2. _____ Do you procrastinate in the hope that problems will go away?

3. _____ When people come to you with problems, do you tell them how to solve them?

4. _____ When confronted with a problem, do you see obstacles rather than possibilities?

5. _____ Are you comfortable asking for help in solving your problems?

6. _____ Do you see how taking a wrong action may be preferable to taking no action at all?

7. _____ When an employee comes to you with a personal problem, do you offer sympathy?

8. _____ Do you trust your intuition in seeking solutions?

9. _____ Do you bring your personal problems to work?

10. _____ Do you allow your employees to "dump" on you emotionally?

11. _____ Do you enjoy the challenge of solving difficult problems?

12. _____ Do you make yourself available to your people to solve all their problems?

13. _____ Do you have a preplanned method for solving problems?

14. _____ Do you seek permanent solutions?

15. _____ Are you aware of your daily cycles, and do you capitalize on them?

Chapter 5

TAKING OVER THE NEW JOB

The initial impression you create when taking over a new job is critical. You must deal with your own apprehensions as well as those of your employees.

Taking Over The New Job

No matter how seasoned you are, there's always some apprehension in taking over a new job. It may be easier to be promoted upward than to change companies, but either way, you know that the initial impression you create is critical.

Carl Gillespie was selected to manage an excelsior plant that had been troubled by labor-management frictions, declining productivity, and poor bottom lines. He arrived promptly at 8:00 A.M. Monday, spent the morning talking with managers and employees, and at noon appeared alone at the company cafeteria where he chatted briefly with several workers and then left to tour the plant. Mid-afternoon, he returned to his office and announced there would be a company-wide employee meeting at 5:00 P.M. As word went throughout the plant, tensions increased noticeably. Some remembered Gillespie as a man who got things done; most had never met him. Everyone waited anxiously as the five o'clock deadline approached.

The meeting lasted barely ten minutes. Carl introduced himself, said that his job was simply *"to get this plant moving again,"* and then made the following announcement: *"This plant will close down at 7:00 P.M. tonight. It will reopen at 8:00 A.M. tomorrow morning, at which time I will be happy to accept employment applications for all positions."* With that, he thanked everyone for coming and bade them goodnight.

People began lining up at the plant gate by 7:30 the next morning. Virtually everyone reapplied, most for their jobs, but some for entirely different positions. Perhaps most interesting was the change in attitudes that took place overnight. Gillespie's simple yet daring move had caused the employees to think about their jobs from a different perspective. While the tension still prevailed, there was an added expectancy that things would get better.

> *Do you become a maintainer of the status quo, or do you strike out to make your own mark?*

Difficult situations, such as that faced by Gillespie, have their plus side; almost any gains will make you look good. But what if you are called to replace a someone who did everything right, who was regarded almost with awe by his co-workers? Do you become a maintainer of the status quo, or do you strike out to make your own mark?

The answers are not always clear, but one thing is certain. Each person has his or her own special place, time, and role. Conditions change rapidly today and with them, the requirements for leadership. No two people face identical challenges or bring exactly comparable views and skills to the job. Your task, in such a situation, is to examine the job and yourself. What has changed? What is likely to change in the future? What can you offer that is truly unique? There's always something, and if you look deeply enough, you'll discover it for yourself.

Regardless of whether you come from the outside or are promoted from within, your reputation precedes you. Your boss, colleagues, and employees watch your every move. You must grasp the reins quickly and firmly, yet still convey an impression of openness, balance, and objectivity. How do you do it?

Attitudes and Approaches

Tough/nice managers are under no illusion that they can slip in unannounced. They know that, right or wrong, word of their coming will have spread. They approach the situation carefully. They begin by gathering as much information as they can about the organization (assuming they come in as an outsider), its people, and the problems. They look for facts rather than opinions and recognize that their initial conclusions can only be tentative and may have to be modified in light of later experience.

Then, based on this initial fact finding, they decide what impression they want to convey. They leave little to chance. Carl Gillespie made his point quickly and forcefully. So did John James, who became president of a closely held midwestern tool company. He had been warned before taking the job that the company treasurer, a major stockholder, had forced two earlier CEOs out. John met privately with the chairman and another key stockholder and was assured that the board would back him in whatever course he chose. On his first day on the job, John ordered the executive parking spaces removed and the occupants' names painted out. When the treasurer arrived at 10:00 A.M. (his usual hour), he was dumbfounded to find a vendor's car parked in his space. This proved to be only the first of several hard lessons he learned. John finally prevailed. Four months later, the treasurer resigned.

Steps

Bold entrances are often effective if you can pull them off. If not, you may be a long time recovering. As a tough/nice manager, you must approach the new job with caution, order, and deliberateness.

1. **Begin by gathering the facts.** Learn about the organization and the job. Find out what has been done well, what problems there are, and what will be expected of you. Be alert for *"nonfacts,"* such as fervently expressed opinions or friendly warnings from those who have axes to grind. Much of what you are told is "fact" may turn out to be rumor or even deliberate misinformation. Study the company's history and the backgrounds of those you'll be working for and with. The more you learn before you arrive, the better prepared you will

be. This all comes under the heading of doing your homework. Surprisingly, many people fail to take this initial step.

2. **Decide what impression you want to convey.** In time, people will see you for what you are, not what you pretend to be. Thus, the manager who goes in with a pretentious style will ultimately be discovered. What works best is to discover and display the genuine you. That's why we've spent so much time on the subject of qualities. Effective managers, and particularly tough/nice managers, know who they are and don't attempt to conceal their identities behind a facade.

3. **Ask questions of everybody, especially employees and colleagues.** Listen, record, and compare what you learn with what you feel and with your predispositions before coming on board. Your early weeks on the job will involve a fair amount of sorting--fact from fiction, significant from insignificant, long term from short term. Curiosity may have killed the cat, but it can also help prevent an astute manager from making fatal mistakes.

4. **Get your boss to set boundaries.** It is imperative to know what is expected of you, what authority you will have, and what support you will get. Many bosses are reluctant to lay it on the line, but it is absolutely essential to your success that they do.

5. **Set your own boundaries.** Boundary setting is a two-way street. We'll be talking more about it in the next chapter, but for now, simply be aware that you must do it, early. Your managers and employees need to know who you are, what you expect of them, and what they can expect from you.

6. **Build mechanisms for feedback.** An open-door policy, frequent informal conversations--what one manager called, *"stopping by"*--and regular rap sessions and lunches are examples. With today's more educated work force, motivation is more a function of communication than direction. Openness rather than authority inspires dedication. Here, we can learn a lesson from the Japanese. Their dogged emphasis on quality circles, flexible job definitions, and broadly based incentive systems reflects a fundamental difference in perspective. Our authority-centered management systems are based on the subconscious assumption that a significant gap exists between

highly qualified leaders and less capable employees. The Japanese approach, on the other hand, seeks to maximize every member's contribution. Communication, down, up, and lateral, is extremely important.

7. **Give feedback.** Have you ever gone to your boss with what you thought was a great idea only to be greeted by stony silence or a mumbled, *"That's fine, now what else did you want?"* Feedback is important. Even computers are trained to respond. Your employees need to know that you are listening, that you care how they feel and are interested in their achievements and welfare. Giving feedback closes the loop, helps maintain balance, and increases your chances of success in the new job.

All this applies to your boss as well. If he or she doesn't meet with you periodically and let you know how you're doing, take the initiative and request a meeting.

*****

One final word of advice: go in tough, with an open mind and a willingness to listen.

Thought Provokers

1. _____ As you think of jobs you've assumed or positions you've been promoted into in the past, do you feel that things went as you expected they would?

2. _____ Did you thoroughly research each new position or job before taking over?

3. _____ Do you feel it is important to be liked by your employees?

4. _____ Do others frequently perceive your management style differently than you do?

5. _____ When you assumed your current position, did your boss define his or her boundaries to you?

6. _____ When you first assumed your position, did you give your employees an opportunity to express their views?

7. _____ Do you have an open-door policy with respect to your employees?

8. _____ Does your boss have a similar policy?

9. _____ Do you consistently follow established policies and procedures yourself?

10. _____ Do you frequently hold formal evaluations with your employees in order to give feedback regarding their progress?

11. _____ Have you been comfortable stipulating tough management policies up front?

Chapter 6

DEFINING YOUR BOUNDARIES

Employees need to know where they stand. Managers who fail to define their requirements and expectations invite confusion and encourage mediocrity.

Defining Your Boundaries

Jack McLeary joined the Recon Corporation in April 1984. Recon, a mid-sized New England industrial optics firm , hired him to replace a vice-president and treasurer who had been summarily fired. In his new job, he inherited nearly a hundred people in accounting, administration, contracting, and data processing.

Jack approached his job carefully. As a member of the management committee, he learned quickly that Recon had problems, many of which fell in his area. Three weekly meetings passed and he said little. He became an enigma to his own people, asking endless questions, and saying little in return. When asked about his reticence by his boss, he explained that it was essential to get a firm fix on the problems before taking any action. When issues arose among his staff, he asked questions and promised to *"look into it."*

Within a month, tensions began to mount. A department head quit without notice. Two senior programmers got into a violent physical dispute in the cafeteria, and Jack's weekly reports began coming out late and error-filled. Jack reacted abruptly. He blamed his managers for not supporting him and vowed to get the culprit who was sabotaging the information system. His relationship with his employees continued to deteriorate. After little more than a year, Jack was history, terminated as abruptly as his predecessor.

What went wrong? The board wanted to know and the president was expected to have answers. There were post mortems to determine why recruiters were paid nearly thirty thousand dollars to bring Jack on board. Slowly the answers emerged.

Jack's first mistake was in approaching the job timidly. He reasoned that his people were already unsettled by his predecessor's abrupt departure and vowed to avoid making waves until he was accepted by his people. In fact, he never was. He failed to establish his boundaries quickly and firmly and, in his failure, created an atmosphere of doubt and innuendo. He created a vacuum that was filled by supposition and innuendo.

Many managers, especially inexperienced ones, fear that moving in firmly and decisively implies insensitivity and closed-mindedness. Actually, the reverse is true. The manager who sets his or her boundaries early forestalls the normal speculations that attend a new arrival and establishes an atmosphere of openness and concern. One who fails to set boundaries risks the almost certain outcome of being misjudged and second-guessed.

We, as managers, can learn from our animal friends— wolves, coyotes, and even dogs and cats. These cunning creatures establish boundaries quickly and repeatedly if need be. They recognize that defining one's bounds provides protection and avoids confusion. Smart managers use boundary setting to determine the limits of acceptable behavior.

Defining one's boundaries is a recurrent task. All new managers or employees need to know where they stand, what they can expect, and what will be expected of them. Most new employees want to contribute and be recognized for what they do. Unfortunately, many managers are like Jack. They fail to communicate early with their employees and establish the mutual bounds within which they will operate. This failure causes employees to be misinformed, confused, and frustrated. They are forced to rely on guess and rumor. Such haphazard familiarization seldom works well. Both sides get off on the wrong foot.

Attitudes and Approaches

Tough/nice managers understand that people are more productive when they know what is expected of them and what they can expect from others. They set boundaries early and act quickly to build understanding and rapport. They leave little to chance and are explicit about themselves, their views, and their requirements.

This early meeting of the minds is especially important for new employees. It does much to relieve the natural apprehension of the first few weeks on the job. It enables them to be more productive, to act more confidently, and to make fewer mistakes. Everyone benefits.

Steps

Defining your boundaries requires deliberate action and great sensitivity. As accomplished by the tough/nice manager, seven steps are involved:

1. **Define your style and expectations--who you are, how you like to work, what you expect from those you manage, and what they can expect of you.** It may help to write out your views in the form of a *"management profile,"* a sample of which is included at the end of this chapter.

2. **Help employees to define their level of responsibility.** *"Do you understand what is expected of you?"* and *"Are you confident that you can do the job?"* are good openers. While the position may be covered by a formal job description, the best situation is when the employee writes down his or her own understanding of the position and responsibilities so that you can both agree on them.

3. **Be sensitive to the employee's training needs and see that they are met.** It's easy to assume that an employee possesses certain skill levels. Don't assume! Ask.

4. **Agree on priorities and deadlines and be sure they are understood.**

5. **Allow the employee the freedom to succeed or fail.** This involves a delicate balance. Too much guidance can frustrate success; too little can cause failure. Yet, failure can be an essential part of the learning process.

6. **Be attentive to sense when an employee needs help, either to assure success or to prevent failure.** Formal evaluations seldom provide sufficiently frequent support mechanisms. A habit of regular communication with all of your people is important to their long-term success.

7. **As new employees increase in skill and confidence, expand their boundaries and responsibilities.** Some managers may object on grounds that, in shifting work to others, they are working themselves out of a job. Actually, that's exactly what should be happening. As managers shed tasks and share responsibilities, they become less commanders and more facilitators, retain their legitimate decision-making powers, and increase their ability to inspire dedication in others.

*****

Think of boundaries as guidelines rather than limits, empowering rather than restricting those who work for you. Your work force is a team, but you are still the team leader.

A SAMPLE MANAGEMENT PROFILE

(This profile represents only one approach to defining your boundaries. You may elect to be less specific or softer, depending upon your managment style and the situation. The important thing, as Jack McLeary found out, is not to leave it to chance.)

WHO I AM

As a manager,

- I am dedicated to developing people and helping them reach their goals.
- I have a record of success achieved in direct proportion to the success of those who work with me.
- I am experienced in all aspects of this business and exposed to the same frustrations and problems that you face.
- I am empathetic rather than sympathetic and know the differences between making attempts and giving excuses.
- I am liberal with strokes, but only in relation to deeds done. Don't expect to receive praise you haven't earned.

>I like strokes also, but I expect to earn them.

>I will treat you as an adult and with respect.

>I will try at all times to be honest and fair.

>I am not reluctant to make decisions.

>I am demanding and supportive.

HOW I LIKE TO WORK

I enjoy working with:

- People who share their knowledge and ideas in order to help the company grow.
- Effective communication networks at all levels.
- People who don't make unwarranted assumptions about individuals or situations before gathering all the facts.

- People who set high standards for themselves and then strive to achieve them.
- People who invite criticism and evaluation--who aren't afraid to look inside themselves and examine their weaknesses.
- People who assume responsibility for their actions.
- People who combine strong inner-based loyalty with respect for others.

WHAT I EXPECT

I expect that you will:

- See yourself as a professional and behave accordingly at all times.
- Lead by example whenever possible.
- Assume responsibility for your actions (decisions and mistakes).
- Communicate your frustrations and disagreements privately to your supervisor or to me.
- Make mistakes--but, learn from them and do not dwell on them.
- Adhere to existing systems and procedures.
- Work with others in a spirit of cooperation.
- Keep your office or work area clean and organized.
- Be on the job when scheduled.

WHAT YOU CAN EXPECT FROM ME

You, in turn can expect that I will:

- Be available when your supervisor isn't, or when you feel you need further support.
- Demand your best in order to help you live up to your fullest potential.
- Provide you with the tools and training necessary to help you function at maximum capacity.

- Take a personal interest in your career and help you attain your goals.

Thought Provokers

1. _____ Do you feel that most employees want to contribute and be recognized as valuable members of the organization?

2. _____ Do you think it's the employee's responsibility to figure out what the job is about?

3. _____ Do you ever do things that create fear in your employees?

4. _____ Would you say that defining your expectations to a new employee creates fear?

5. _____ Do you think it is important to define your management style to those who work for you?

6. _____ Do your associates always know how you will react in a given situation?

7. _____ Do you allow your employees to make mistakes?

8. _____ Do you take positive steps to create awareness in your employees?

9. _____ Do you demand that they take responsibility for their actions?

10. _____ Are you alert to their needs?

11. _____ Do you gain agreement on priorities and deadlines?

12. _____ Do you find that you constantly adjust your level of expectation with some employees?

13. _____ Are you comfortable placing demands on your employees?

14. _____ Do you willingly share knowledge with others employees, coworkers, and bosses?

15. _____ Should you always be available to your employees?

16. _____ Do you take personal interest in each of your employees' careers?

17. _____ Do you encourage your employees to assist in each other's development?

Chapter 7

BUILDING INNER-BASED LOYALTY

The best employees are loyal to them-selves first and to their companies second.

Building Inner-Based Loyalty

Three vice-presidents from Sports Limited sat at lunch discussing their respective loyalties to the company and its president, Rob Hagan.

Jean, the oldest of the three, began: *"I've been with this company nearly seven years, and I've had my share of lean paychecks and long hours. Now, with this new expansion, the revised pay system, and the plans to go public, I think things will get better. And besides, I'm fifty-two and I'm not prepared to go out job-hunting again if I can avoid it."* Phil, ten years younger and financially more successful than Jean, continued: *"I agree. This company's on the move. I believe what Mr. Hagan has said. If we just stick together, we can all make lots of money."* He stopped, averted his gaze from Jean, who had been nodding in agreement. He turned to Cam, the youngest and yet most senior member of the trio, and said, *"Cam, you've been here longer than we have. How do you see it?"*

"Not the way you do," Cam replied. *"I'll stay with this company only as long as I feel I am growing and being challenged. So far that's been the case, but I have to tell you, I think that's changing. This business is cyclical, and right now we're having a hard time. Failures are*

higher than ever before. I don't trust Rob Hagan. I think he's using the company to further his own ends and salt away enough so that he can walk from it. I've heard so much of this PMA (Positive Mental Attitude) crap the past fifteen years that I've had it up to here. My first loyalty is to myself, my own growth, and survival. You both know that because we are in a sales business that we operate as independent profit centers pitted against each other. So my second loyalty is to my people. They're the ones who make it all happen. My third loyalty is to this company, because I feel it is us, *not the company, that make the difference. I think that Mr. Hagan and his inner group work to maintain a steady edge of competitive jealousy among us, and when we fail to comply, they will force us out."*

Pretty tough words, aren't they? Who is right? Jean, for whom the company is a haven; Phil, who trusts his boss and believes that big rewards are just around the corner; or Cam, the most skeptical? As it turned out, Cam's prediction was right in just about every respect. The fortunes of the company went down, not up, and in the year preceding its demise Rob Hagan personally took out over a million dollars in compensation.

Many of those displaced in today's turbulent job market have discovered something tough/nice managers have known for a long time: in all too many cases, company loyalty is a form of leverage to get people to behave in certain ways. In good times, when things were going well, this kind of manipulation worked. There were always promises of big things to come. Now, with massive layoffs and restructuring, the litany of loyalty to the company falls on deaf ears. The emphasis is on current rewards--big bucks today with no assurances about tomorrow.

This isn't all bad. There's another side to the story. Many companies caught up in the race for growth have confused loyalty with performance. Riding the bandwagon rather than pushing it has become acceptable. Too many managers have attempted to hide in over-staffed support functions, to poke their heads out occasionally and cheer the others on. And too many managers have encouraged the nonsense of excess layering.

The fact is, you can demand performance but you must inspire loyalty. Traditional wisdom has it that company loyalty comes first. That is seldom true. Bobbie Cooke, a member of The Group, Inc. says of loyalty, *"I'm loyal to this company because I feel our goals are compatible. It offers me opportunities I can't provide for myself. In turn, I produce. I am dedicated to becoming continually better, and I'm working here with others who have the same goal."*

Many companies mistakenly assume they can demand loyalty from their employees. The inevitable result is a heterogeneous mix of people biding their time and using the organization for their own ends. In the short run, this disparity may be unapparent but in the long run it shows up.

Excellent companies build for the long term. They are astute enough to recognize that the philosophies and goals they espouse must be compatible with those of the people they employ. These companies attract outstanding individuals who possess a deep inner loyalty to themselves and a special sense of mission. These self-motivated individuals deliver extraordinary performance because they are able to perceive a compatibility between their own and their company's goals.

Attitudes and Approaches

Tough/nice managers are realistic. They help their employees attain their goals within the context of the corporate mission. Yet they realize that the corporation's goals must come first. They understand, therefore, that they must sense the different aspirations of their employees and unify their efforts in a common direction. They build loyalty by earning respect for their ability, integrity, and fairness. They recognize full well that loyalty cannot be demanded; it must be won.

The tough side of tough/nice managers enables them to recognize that demanding the best of their employees may involve a struggle. Even the best employees must occasionally be pushed to exceed their own limits. This tough and visionary aspect of their management style results in a consistently higher percentage of outstanding employees. Their toughness also allows them to act quickly when they sense a basic incompatibility between an employee's goals and those of the corporation.

Steps

Building loyalty requires time, sustained effort, and sensitivity. Six steps are involved:

1. **Establish your boundaries immediately and communicate them clearly.**

2. **Determine what each employee expects from the company and what the employee is willing to give.**

3. **Learn to harness energy and diversity in building your management team.**

(a) Understand each member's strengths, weaknesses, attitudes, and aspirations.

(b) Determine how each person can best contribute (remember that negative people can often spot pitfalls that optimists ignore).

(c) Outline the tasks and gain commitment from each member.

(d) Build mechanisms to encourage open communications, resolve differences, and jointly appraise results, that is, an open door policy, regular formal and informal meetings with your people.

4. **Be clear, fair, and consistent in your dealings.** Loyalty depends on respect, not friendship.

5. **Don't retreat when challenged if you know you're right.** You weren't elected by popular vote; you were appointed because you proved you could do the job.

6. **Be realistic about what you expect.** Learn to assess accurately others' capabilities and dedication. You cannot want success for them more than they want it for themselves.

*****

In some organizations, company loyalty is a sensitive issue. Conflicts between organizational loyalty and one's personal values ultimately undermine productivity.

Thought Provokers

1. _____ Do you find it difficult to make commitments and keep them?

2. _____ Do you frequently break agreements with yourself?

3. _____ Do you give as much respect as you demand from others?

4. _____ Do you often put others' needs ahead of your own?

5. _____ Do you expect others to be loyal to you because of your position?

6. _____ Are you willing to work with a capable subordinate who has indicated a lack of commitment to the company?

7. _____ Do you feel a conflict between loyalty to yourself and loyalty to your organization?

8. _____ Do you sometimes sacrifice your standards in order to gain others' loyalty?

9. _____ Do your coworkers confide in you or ask for your advice?

10. _____ Do you regularly praise your employees for their accomplishments?

11. _____ Do you sometimes go overboard with praise or rewards?

12. _____ Do you assign work equitably among your employees according to their skills, training, and position?

13. _____ Are you clear as to the appropriate balance between your employees' accomplishments and the praise you give them?

Chapter 8

MANAGING UP--CREATING OPPORTUNITY FOR YOURSELF

Tough/nice managers make their boss a winner
because they can't afford to spend time with losers.

Managing Up--Creating Opportunity For Yourself

Managing up is, for many, an unnatural act. You're expected to respond to your boss's demands and manage your own people. You are not expected to manage your boss. Yet that is just what tough/nice managers do. They make their boss look good and protect him or her when necessary, while still safeguarding their own interests and those of their employees and the company.

Managing up can be difficult, as Hal Crow and Charlie Watman learned. Both regarded their boss, Fred Peterson, as excessively aloof and as a man possessed with his own private agenda. Hal had been with Raneer Electronics for over ten years. His division accounted for more than 60 percent of corporate sales, and he was well regarded within the company and the industry. Hal felt that Peterson was inept and went around him wherever possible so he avoided outright confrontation except when he felt the customer's or his people's interests were at stake. He set his boss aside, ran the division as a company within a company, and seemed resigned to the situation. When prodded, his only response was, *"Some dogs are just too old to change."*

Charlie held a somewhat different position. While he shared Hal's views about their boss, he made every effort to make Peterson look good. He included him in major customer briefings and kept him abreast of goings on within his division.

Managing up is a joint activity. If your boss refuses to be managed, is incompetent, or is hopelessly arrogant, managing up can be a losing battle. Let's look at it from a different viewpoint, that of a manager who demanded that her managers manage up. Clarissa Payne headed up a division of a large eastern sales organization. Sixteen managers reported to her. She not only expected that her managers manage up, she demanded it. She is definite in her views:

> *People are empowered by their willingness to assume responsibility for their actions.*

> There's an old saying that applies to organizations generally, that I have applied to my division: "A chain is only as strong as its weakest link." My division is only as strong as each person in it. That includes every position, from the top down. People are empowered by their willingness to assume responsibility for their actions. Awareness and cooperation are keys to making it happen, but there's no way for a person to be aware of everything. We have to rely on others to make us more aware, and we must be willing to listen and to set aside our egos.

> Many bosses will not take suggestions from their subordinates. They either believe that they have all the answers by virtue of their positions, or they're afraid they might appear incompetent if they accept advice from an employee. Still other managers rely on fear or power to motivate and keep their employees in line.

> I train my employees to manage up. First, I give them permission--to question, challenge, and advise. Second, I make them aware that it is their responsibility to speak up. Often, if they've come from a highly authoritarian atmosphere, they're uncomfortable at first. They see me as the authority and are afraid to challenge. In time, however, they recognize that it is their responsibility to help create awareness at all levels in the organization. They learn not to be the weakest link.

> I train my people to ask themselves two questions, and they're questions I ask constantly: "What am I doing that is causing a problem?" and "What can I do that will be more helpful?" Everyone recognizes these as key questions, and this recognition encourages the kind of openness that builds strength within an organization. I know that my own willingness to open up has created tremendous respect from my people. In addition, I am constantly learning.

> This process of managing up begins with the new sales trainee. Everyone in this division is taught to speak up, question, challenge and--in appropriate ways--to blow off steam if necessary. The result is that even new sales people and inexperienced managers develop self-esteem and confidence more quickly. They are more relaxed about taking risks and more open in sharing their concerns. There is less bickering and arguing, and we tend to regard one another as parts of a support network. This applies even when our people compete for sales. They know, because they've seen it work, that cooperation rather than competition is the key to their long-term success. And it works for me too. I don't feel the pressure to throw my weight around, because I know I can count on

everyone to jump in and work their tails off when the going gets tough. I'm also aware
that if I'm off base, someone will let me know.

Clarissa's style seems to have paid off. The tasks of delegation
appear to have been simplified immensely, since her people are con-
ditioned to look continually for ways to assume more responsibility.
Her division, moreover, has consistently been a leader in sales, and
she has routinely turned out better managers than either of the other
two divisions in the company. For her, managing up works.

Attitudes and Approaches

For many, managing up represents a change in perspective.
Tough/nice managers see themselves as entrepreneurs as well.
They view success as a result of their own efforts, but recognize that
they must be supported from below and above. They are equally concerned that their employees and their boss are winners. They see
themselves as facilitators for those below and catalysts for those
above. Larry Kendall put it well when he said that a major task was
to be certain that he didn't get in his people's way. Consistently,
tough/nice managers recognize the importance of managing up--by
accepting it from their people and practicing it on their boss.

Steps

Managing up may not come naturally at first, for it violates traditional ideas about command and control. With practice, you'll
see that it works and that it's an effective way of maximizing the
resources of your organization. There are several steps involved:

1. **Set your own goals and decide whether you can achieve
them within the company.** If after careful consideration you decide
you cannot, your next action should be obvious!

2. **Know your boss.** Study the person. Learn what motivates what
frightens, or angers your boss, what is expected of you, what your
boss is willing and able to give, and how receptive he or she is to suggestions and criticism.

3. **Make yourself indispensable.** Of course, no one is totally indispensable, but you can at least become difficult to replace:

(a) Help your employees become winners. Give them all the challenge and autonomy they can handle. Teach them to manage up, too.

(b) Become a center of influence for your peers. Learn how your job relates to theirs and how you can help them.

(c) Practice seeing problems from your boss's viewpoint. Learn to suggest alternative ways of solving them.

4. **Develop your own vision of your company's future, its mission, goals, and objectives.** Think how your vision could become a reality. Vision is critical to success. It adds perspective and helps you focus on possibilities rather than limits.

5. **Practice turning disagreements into consensus, and consensus into action.** Use your questioning skills. Ask questions rather than making statements. In this way, you become mediator and facilitator rather than threat, someone who can be counted on to tackle the tough problems and come up with imaginative solutions.

6. **Be willing to take risks when they offer the potential for significant gains without the probability of catastrophic losses.** Spend money to make money. Opportunities just over the horizon may not be visible or fundable through normal channels. You may have to resort to untraditional means to launch your best ideas.

7. **Let your actions speak first, and if necessary, be sure that the words follow.** If your boss is short on recognition and long on demands, ask questions that highlight your achievements. Keep a record of what you've accomplished. Know how good you are and be ready to prove it!

*****

Tough/nice managers are not "yes men." They will risk disapproval when they feel a redirection of thinking or approach is needed. They are tough-minded and realistic about their own and their company's success.

Thought Provokers

1. _____ Do you take full responsibility for your success?

2. _____ Are you sensitive to your boss's needs, motivations, and goals?

3. _____ Are your goals compatible with those of your company?

4. _____ Do you consistently do things to make yourself indispensable?

5. _____ Do you have a vision of your company's future?

6. _____ Are you a center of influence for your peers?

7. _____ Do you make an offer to see problems from your boss's point of view?

8. _____ Do you spend your own money to further your education or training?

9. _____ Are you regarded by others as being solution oriented?

10. _____ Does upper-level management solicit your ideas?

11. _____ Do you praise your peers when they deserve it?

12. _____ Do you volunteer for special assignments that will provide more growth or recognition than you could get from the routines of your job?

Chapter 9

TAKING RISKS

*Employees who refuse to take risks impede
their own and their company's growth. Employees
who take risks foolishly endanger their own and
their company's future. It is upon the shoulders
of those who risk intelligently that the success
of the company rests.*

Taking Risks

M anagers are risk takers, right? Wrong. Where possible, most managers avoid risks, preferring instead the comforts of secure employment, regular promotions, and dependable retirement. Now, in the wake of widespread reorganizations and layoffs, many of these scenarios are not working. Consider the evidence:

- Upwards of a million managers and workers have lost their jobs within the past three years. For many displaced in the shuffle, finding another job has meant lengthy unemployment, significant retraining, reduced pay, and career changes.

- Many displaced managers find jobs in newer, smaller companies, and it is in the 750,000 new start-ups each year that most growth is occurring. The catch is that these new companies involve even greater risks. Some estimates have it that up to half of them will fail within two years.

- Organizations are demanding more and promising less. It's a buyer's market in many industries. The sudden proliferation of front-loaded compensation schemes, contract employment, and cross-training requirements is a sign that the myth of promised security has been shattered.

Sources of the current dilemma have been apparent for some time. Increases in foreign competition, a preference for quantity over quality, and the inappropriateness of many management approaches have been obvious for at least a decade. Many companies have refused to adapt. Belatedly, they have become concerned with quality, but only when it has an immediate effect on profits. For many firms, long-range planning seldom extends beyond the next quarterly report.

We have created an age of impossible superlatives in which no achievement is quite good enough and in which "more" rather than "better" is sought. Managers, caught in the middle, have reacted. Some have dug in, adopted a conservative approach, and tried to weather the storm. Others have risked their own and their company's futures foolishly. Still others have dropped out. The unfortunate result is that everyone seems to be playing catch-up and no one is sure of the outcome.

This myopia is largely the result of three failures that affect a majority of organizations and their managers.

1. The failure to recognize that risk is essential for growth. Jack Turner is an expert mountain climber, philosopher, and computer whiz who has lived and climbed in Nepal and now teaches climbing in Wyoming's Grand Tetons. He tells about Leland, a twelve-year old who enrolled in a

> *"Courage takes place only in the presence of fear. Without fear, there is no need for courage."*
>
> Jack Turner - subject of fear

beginner's course. Leland was so terrified when faced with his first ascent that he began to hyperventilate, even though the rock was only slightly taller than he was. Each time it was the same. *"I can't do it,"* he would gasp. The other kids were justifiably cynical, but Jack refused to let him quit. Slowly, over several hours, Leland began to change. He not only managed the afternoon's rappel, he returned the next day for the intermediate course! According to Jack, for many people it is tenacity rather than ability that enables them to succeed.

Managers who have survived during the past five years will echo Jack's sentiments. It's the tough assignments and their attendant risks that promote growth.

2. The failure to distinguish between real and perceived risk. Colorado Outward Bound School (COBS) teaches managers how to separate the two. Stephen McCormick, Director of Professional Development for COBS, tells about the "wall" and the "ropes," two tests their manager-students undergo. By the time the managers confront these challenges, they are so aware of the school's safety precautions that they know there is little physical danger. They discover that it is not fear of falling but of failing in front of their peers that matters. In learning to face their real fears, the managers develop inner courage and a sense of how important the support of others can be. As Jack Turner put it, *"Courage takes place only in the presence of fear. Without fear, there is no need for courage."*

3. The failure to risk intelligently. Gamblers and intelligent risk takers are usually miles apart. It's not beating the odds but increasing the certainty of the outcome that counts. Managers who serve their organizations well are careful and thorough in their approach to risk. They know what they want to achieve and are aware of the factors that can cause them to fail, as well as those that enable them to succeed. They know how far to go and avoid endangering themselves or their organization unnecessarily.

Attitudes and Approaches

Tough/nice managers are realists. They know that taking risks is part of their job. When a chancy situation arises, they don't ask, "Why did this happen to me?" Instead, they view it as an opportunity to grow and assume responsibility for the outcome. They refuse to accept chance as a deciding factor, because they see themselves as being in control. Their outlook, attitudes, and habitual way of approaching problems give them a sense of tactical readiness--a conviction that "whatever happens, I can handle it."

Steps

How can you develop the tough/nice manager's tactical readiness and improve your risk-taking skills? For most managers, the process involves changes in attitude and habit. There are four principal steps:

1. **Accept risk and change as necessary.** This acceptance begins as an act of faith that is confirmed through experience. There are certain signs, however, that may encourage you to take this step. Look at the steel and auto companies that have attempted to resist change and avoid risk. What has been the result? How successful have they been?

Once you take the plunge and accept risk as a fact of work and life, you free yourself to undergo a change of perspective. You become more calm and detached because you are able to recognize risk taking as essential to your overall development. Furthermore, you begin to realize something that the tough/nice manager knows: most risk situations are metaphors that offer lessons far beyond the immediate crisis.

2. **Learn to distinguish between real and apparent risks.** The real risks are seldom evident at first glance. Clarity of perception is clouded by fear, belief, prejudice, and expectation. Additionally, in those early moments of taking stock, there's been no opportunity to assess the real risks in any organized way. All too often, what you feel is a product of predispositions that have preceded the actual event. So your first task is to begin asking some tough questions, such as: What most worries or frightens me about this situation? How valid are my fears? Are any of my beliefs or prejudices (yes, we all have them) coloring my judgment? Am I holding out certain expectations that may not be justified or necessary? Answering these questions for yourself helps uncover the misconceptions most of us harbor, and reveals the often vast gulf between real and perceived risks.

3. **Anticipate what can cause you to fail.** Most managers have been instilled, by training and experience, with what might be called a *"success orientation." "What do I have to do in order to make it?"* is the question that marks this attitude. They have been discouraged

from asking negative questions, such as *"What might cause me to fail?"* Yet tough/nice managers do just that, for they know that there are usually more factors that can cause failure than will ensure success. The difference between the two types of questions is not just a semantic distinction. Asking a negative question is an approach used in a highly sophisticated discipline called *"failure analysis"* and differs greatly from asking positive ones. A simple way to use failure analysis is to add to your normal success-based question, ones such as the following:

(a) What factors might cause me to fail?

(b) How likely are they to occur?

(c) If they do occur, how will that affect the situation?

(d) What can I do to prevent them from occurring?

(e) If they occur, what can I do about it?

Don't assume that asking these questions will cause you to become negative about the situation. In fact, the reverse is the case. This process, when practiced consistently, helps you develop the tactical readiness we mentioned earlier. In learning to anticipate all possible outcomes, you are prepared for whatever happens and much less surprised and fearful if and when it does!

4. **Encourage risk taking in others.** If you are willing to take risks, your employees will follow suit. Conversely, if you attempt to avoid all risks, you'll find that those around you will try to avoid risky assignments and difficult decisions. Your actions will prove contagious to others. Intelligent risk taking and innovative enterprise go hand-in-hand.

One thing more. Mistakes and occasional failures are an inevitable part of the learning process. By encouraging those around you to take risks, you are admitting that you recognize and accept that they will make mistakes.

*****

Companies on the move offer high-risk situations and opportunities for fast learning. Lethargic companies offer low risk and provide little growth.

Thought Provokers

1._____ Do you avoid situations involving new people or unfamiliar surroundings?

2._____ When confronted with a problem or unfortunate incident, do you wonder, "Why did this happen to me?"

3._____ Do you feel that much of your life is a matter of chance?

4._____ Are you calm and collected when confronted with a crisis situation?

5._____ When you make a mistake or a poor decision, does it nag you for days?

6._____ Do you feel that you are a risk taker?

7._____ Are you content with the extent to which you are willing to take risks?

8._____ Do you encourage others to take risks?

9._____ Would you promote an employee who avoids taking risks?

10. _____ Do you have a disciplined approach to analyzing risks?

11._____ Do you feel that it's possible to spread the risk and still achieve the objective?

12._____ Do you find that you sometimes ignore the risks?

Chapter 10

MANAGING YOUR MANAGERS

*Most managers would rather direct than teach,
but in the long run it is teaching that builds
the organization.*

Managing Your Managers

M anagers are teachers, but in a very special way. Perhaps *"facilitators"* would be a better word, for they teach by ex- ample, questions, suggestions, and--sparingly--by instruction. The manager's role is always to encourage others to think for themselves. As first-level supervisors, their emphasis is on individual perfor- mance. Above entry level, however, they teach supervisors to become managers and teachers. Their task is complicated by the fact that some performers may never become good managers and that many managers lack an aptitude for teaching. Thus, the manager's task is to select and develop those with the greatest potential.

The task is further complicated by two additional factors: the manager's own perspective and the people he or she inherits. Often new managers are more concerned with the transition from doing to directing than with the need to develop others. They forget that they are a model for those who report to them and that employees will emulate or reject what they do depending on how those employees perceive them.

Whether promoted from within or imported from outside the or- ganization, most managers inherit the majority of those who report to them. They are often confronted, therefore, with significant differences in management style and operating practices. As a result, they must decide how much conformity they will require.

Strong managers can influence those who work for them in significant ways. Many succumb to the enticements of ego and surround themselves with people who think the same way and who have comparable operating styles. If they are not careful, they can create serious problems for themselves and their ogranizations.

Carla Boyd is a case in point. She started at the bottom of a growing consumer-products company, quickly became manager of an ailing sales outlet, and turned it around within thirty days. Two years later, she could boast of eight other successful turnarounds. Within five years, she became a regional supervisor with a dozen managers reporting to her. Carla was a strong leader who believed in the virtues of training. She designed and taught her own training program and pushed her people in the right directions. They responded by imitating her obviously successful operating style. At one training session, she had her managers complete a self-assessment exercise known as the Myers-Briggs Type Indicator. The MBTI, as it is called, measures individual preferences with respect to four indices: extraversion-introversion, sensing-intuition (perceiving styles), thinking-feeling (judging styles), and preferences with respect to the styles themselves. The results were not surprising. Three-quarters of Carla's managers' scores turned out to be very close to her own. In a field where extraverts often prevail (sales), she and most of her managers were introverts. In addition, there was a striking similarity in their perceiving and judging styles.

> *The manager's role is always to encourage others to think for themselves.*

Initially, Carla was pleased. The results seemed to validate her strong leadership style and extensive training efforts. As she became more familiar with the concepts underlying the assessment, however, Carla realized that something was amiss. Her managers had comparable strengths, but they also had similar weaknesses. She had achieved strong teamwork at a sacrifice of independence. Carla responded by changing her tactics, targeting the individual weaknesses of each manager, and--by training, assignments, and counseling--helping the managers to become more well-rounded. The result was a more balanced management team in which individual differences were encouraged and appreciated.

Carla's experience illustrates an important difference in managers. Strong, confident managers recognize and encourage individual differences as a means of ensuring balance. Weak managers often lack the inner-directedness and intuition necessary to recognize differences in individual preferences, strengths, and weaknesses. They are more comfortable creating clones who

> *Strong managers create an atmosphere of controlled chaos in which individual differences are encouraged.*

think alike and follow rather than lead. Faye Arens, one of Carla's peers, illustrates the point. Faye's region was somewhat larger than Carla's, although her revenues were comparable. She differed from Carla in several critical respects. She kept a tight rein on her managers, delegated only the most menial tasks, and managed by threat and intimidation. For a while, record revenues and profits masked developing problems. Over time, however, several of Faye's managers tired of her style and succeeded in getting transferred elsewhere within the company. These lateral moves were largely unsuccessful. Her managers found they could not hold their own in situations where they were called upon to operate independently and exercise their own judgment. Several left the company frustrated and angry.

Faye's situation is not uncommon. Developing truly resourceful managers requires a willingness to relinquish power and to tolerate diversity. Weak managers demand conformity. Strong managers create an atmosphere of controlled chaos in which individual differences are encouraged. The most astute manage to surround themselves with people who are brighter than themselves in certain areas are and who bring different pespectives to bear.

Attitudes and Approaches

The developmental style of tough/nice managers is closer to Carla's than Faye's. They see themselves as facilitators whose purpose, to quote again from Larry Kendall, is *"to be certain that I don't get in my people's way."* Regardless of their reputation or track record, tough/nice managers see themselves as equally involved in the learning process with their managers. They view their own experience as the raw material from which lessons for others can be developed. At the same time, they recognize that they are still one step removed from the problems faced by those they teach. They are, therefore, sensitive to what they need to learn, particularly in situations where they inherit an existing management staff. They are open and receptive to new ideas, yet have a clear sense of what they want to achieve with their managers. While they accept and welcome differences in attitude, style, and operating practices, they consciously mold their management team along clearly conceived lines. If the managers they develop have any common ground, it is this: independence of thought, dedication to doing their best, and confidence that they can succeed. They are winners in their own right.

Steps

In developing your managers, it is important that you convey confidence and openness and show that you know where you are going. Whether it is a new or ongoing situation, you must act decisively. Ten steps are involved:

1. **Position yourself.** Study your situation. Get your boss's perspective. If you have been moved into the job, talk to others and gather information on the people and the unit. Learn to separate fact from legend. You will find that not everything you'll be told will be accurate.

2. **Establish rapport.** If you've been promoted up, your reputation will have preceded you. If you're moving into a new organization from outside, your task will be somewhat different. You might want to follow this approach to get on top of the job:

(a) Meet with your managers individually and encourage each one to share his or her feelings.

(b) Establish your boundaries quickly (chapter 6).

(c) If you encounter defensiveness, deal with it directly. Ask questions designed to surface problems.

(d) Enlist your managers' cooperation in reaching solutions to obvious problems.

(e) Gain agreement from your managers as to the commitments they are willing to make.

3. **Develop working hypotheses.** In any new situation, you will sense things you can't prove--attitudes or conditions that you feel but just can't pin down. You can avoid snap judgments by formulating hypotheses that can be tested later. Determine what facts you will need to prove or disprove these hypotheses, and develop them over time. This simple device will help prevent you from getting off on the wrong foot and making costly misjudgments.

4. **Develop an action plan.** Set objectives. Determine how much support you will require from others. Give them the tools and training they need. Be concise and direct in assigning responsibilities. Make sure they understand you and then follow up to see that your directions are carried out. Finally, give and require feedback.

5. **Evaluate results in light of your hypotheses.** Were your hunches right? Have things worked out as expected? If not, why? What changes should you make in your attitudes and management style or in your assignments to others. Remember, you may be the manager and teacher, but you can learn from every experience.

6. **Make the necessary changes.** If you goof, admit it and move on. Don't dwell on your mistakes. If you are making major changes, explain why they are necessary and how they will impact on others? Gain agreement by involving those who will be affected. Getting their involvement can be tricky. You need their support, but you want them to recognize that you bear full responsibility for your decisions.

7. **Recognize that your managers play multiple roles.** They perform, direct, delegate, counsel, and teach just as you do. Appraise their total performance. Do they function well in each of these roles? Are they assuming responsibility for their own development? Do they know how to accommodate and utilize differences within their own staffs? Do they seek challenge for themselves and provide it for their people?

8. **Be willing to relinquish power.** Remember Faye Arens's ill-fated example. Often, you must give up power in order for your managers to discover their own strengths. Even though you relinquish authority in certain instances, your people still look to you for over-all leadership.

9. **Encourage diversity.** If everyone on your staff thinks alike, you are unlikely to have a dynamic innovative organization. Your task is to surround yourself with the best people you can find and stimulate them to grow and produce. Strong managers are not intimidated by excellence in others.

10. **Provide Opportunities for cross-training, communication, and interraction.** The more people know about each other and about their respective jobs, the more likely they are to bond in mutually productive ways. A willingness to share knowledge and to communicate openly is an essential perrequisite to successful team accomplishment.

*****

Expect to be challenged. If you are doing your job well, you are developing managers who have minds of their own and who will not be *"yes men."*

Thought Provokers

1._____ Do you delegate responsibility as often as you should?

2._____ Are you receptive to new ideas from your managers?

3._____ Do you see yourself as a teacher?

4._____ Do you generally ask questions before giving instructions?

5._____ When assigned to a new position, do you have a well thought-out approach for gaining control?

6._____ Do you record your first impressions of a new manager or situation and check them later to see if you were right?

7._____ Do you have an action plan for developing your managers?

8._____ Do you lead by example?

9._____ Can you cite instances where your managers have followed the example you have set?

10._____ When you goof, are you comfortable admitting it?

11._____ Do you make a conscious attempt to provide growth experiences for your managers?

12._____ Do you find yourself rescuing them when they really don't need it?

13._____ Do you occasionally allow your managers to fail?

14._____ Are you comfortable ridding yourself of duties that others can perform?

Chapter 11

ENCOURAGING HIGH ACHIEVERS

High achievers cannot be managed in the traditional sense. They are mavericks with their own demands for freedom and opportunity. They require special handling.

Encouraging High Achievers

In most organizations, average performers outnumber high achievers four-to-one. With tradition and standards tending to favor the majority, average performance becomes the norm. Managers adapt their expectations to fit and the inevitable result is that incentive systems are used to reward results that are little better than average.

At least that's the way it was until recently. Beginning four or five years ago, things started to change. Growing economic pressures in many sectors forced a reexamination of the subject of performance. What has been acceptable as average in the past could now no longer be tolerated. The pressure to excel was on. Innovative organizations, their managers, and professional researchers began asking some rather piercing questions:

Why do some people perform consistently better than others despite identical systems for managing, motivating, and compensating?

• How different are these high achievers, and what accounts for the differences?

- What can be done to raise the levels of performance of the 80 percent who are not high achievers?

The answers, tentative at first and gradually more sure, were somewhat surprising. One fact became strikingly apparent. High achievers are strongly inner-directed. Their performance, at least in the short run, is often unrelated to the incentives used to motivate them. They are self-motivated and value-driven.

A second finding was this: the high achievers' preoccupation with performance extends to all areas of their lives. They see a connectedness in all that they do and, as a result, are better able to balance the competing pressures of work, family, education, and leisure. They manage these often divisive forces with a seeming effortlessness that suggests deep inner calm and purpose.

These perceptions prompted a reassessment of the concept of high achievement. Achievement typically has been defined in competitive terms, that, is the high achiever is the one who surpasses others and comes out on top. But often this perspective is not shared by the achievers. They see themselves in a broader context. Their goal is not winning, but mastery. They are people who perform consistently at the upper limits of their abilities and who constantly attempt to expand those limits.

If you're beginning to suspect that there is a parallel between the tough/nice manager and the high achiever, you're right. The tough/nice manager is a high achiever, and both have an intense, qualitative orientation toward life. The high achiever possesses the tough/nice manager's strong inner- directedness and balance, as well as flexibility, power, and commitment.

Let's return to the second question above: How are high achievers different? Researchers have discovered that the distance between average performers and high achievers is much less than we thought. Furthermore, the differences are more in attitude than ability. Many stunningly successful people are by many measures less intelligent, less educated, and less privileged than those around them. Yet, somehow, they prevailed, surpassed their peers, and set new levels for themselves and others to aspire to.

Attitude is the key. The attitudes of high achievers stem directly from the inner qualities they possess. There is a consistency between the way they see themselves and how they perform. Those around them notice the inner confidence, the willingness to accept responsibility, the sense of control, the readiness to deal with whatever comes, and the strong inner drive to excel. The major difference in attitude, however, is that high achievers <u>see</u> themselves as high achievers.

These attitudes are reflected in their *"practices"*, their consciously developed habits. Again, the practices of high achievers are evident to those around them--their penchant for questioning, their need to test their own limits, their willingness to act on intuition, and their commitment to being fully fit. High achievers appear always to be in training, yet they enjoy life. They approach people and situations with curiosity, caring, and humor. They refuse to take themselves or others too seriously.

If there is one characteristic that distinguishes the high achiever from others, it is awareness. High achievers are simply more aware--of the qualities that make them what they are, of the importance of their attitudes and practices, and of the skills that enable them to relate effectively to the world around them. Awareness, for high achievers, is both an attitude and a skill. Their path to high achievement consists of long stretches of diligent alert effort punctuated by sudden breakthroughs in accomplishment. They understand the complex interplay of qualities, skills, attitudes, and practices because they are highly aware--open to new information, reluctant to prejudge, and committed to their own and others' growth.

Attitudes and Approaches

The job of tough/nice managers is made easier by the fact that they are high achievers. They know the difference between average and outstanding performance. Their task is twofold. First, they must create an environment in which high achievers can thrive, and then they must address the question posed earlier: "What can be done to raise the performance of those who are not high achievers?" The methods they use to approach the task are different in each instance.

High achievers cannot be managed in the traditional sense. They have the inclination and discipline required to succeed. They must be nurtured, encouraged, and supported. With a cast of high achievers, the tough/nice manager's role is that of facilitator rather than director, to guide carefully and admonish gently.

The 80 percent who are not high achievers must be managed. The tough/nice manager's task is to bring out their best when they may be unable to see it themselves. This involves a shift in awareness, from the acceptance of limits to a perception of real capabilities. Often there is resistance. People who are unaware of their potential fear change. People who have long been labled as being *"only average"* tend to believe it, and feel that they are incapable of changing. They are so accustomed to thinking in terms of *"I can't"* that it takes a while for them to begin thinking, *"I can."* With these people especially--the majority--managers must be both tough and nice, patient and demanding. It is crucial that the managers' demands be positive, reflecting their conviction that their people can do better. They must keep in mind what high achievement really is and must remember that, in the final analysis, the most meaningful index of performance is the extent to which an individual is working up to and pushing beyond his or her own limits.

Steps

As a manager, your task is to identify, encourage, inspire, and promote high achievement in your organization. An obvious place to begin is to recognize high-achievement characteristics in yourself and provide a model others will want to emulate. Beyond this, there are several steps you can take:

1. **Learn to recognize high achievement traits in others.** Study the five qualities discussed in chapter 1. See how they fit the concept of high achievement and what attitudes and practices follow naturally from them.

(a) **Inner-directedness.** A willingness to be introspective, a strong sense of purpose, high self-esteem, an intense curiosity, and a need to test authorities

(b) **Balance.** An inner stability or centeredness, effective work/life management practices, an ability to see opposing sides of issues, and a conviction that there are always options

(c) **Flexibility.** An ability to accept the unexpected and to change course quickly, a willingness to admit mistakes and avoid blaming others, and a realistic, internally based optimism

(d) **Power.** Poise, a sense of being in control, a willingness to accept (and reject) responsibility, and a tendency to attract others

(e) **Commitment.** Clear direction, dedication, and sustained effort.

2. **Identify current and potential high achievers.** Encourage those in the first group and manage those in the second. Be sure that your expectations for each group are realistic, but don't adjust them downward to accommodate the average and mediocre. Make positive demands for performance.

3. **Don't confuse ability and preference.** Many people have the ability to excel but prefer not to. In most cases, it is preference rather than ability that determines whether they will succeed or fail. Pinpoint those who want to succeed, and weed out those who don't. A winning environment is one in which there is a strong shared drive to succeed.

4. **Channel your people's efforts.** As the boss, your position gives you a perspective others may lack. Even high achievers need guidance. You can inspire, challenge, guide, and coordinate the high achievers. You can shield them from the often wasteful games of office politics, and you can see that they have what they need to do the job.

5. **Reward your people's accomplishments.** Giving visible recognition to high achievers (and potential high achievers) lets everyone know that there are incentives for excellence. High achievers are often poorly used. Their obvious genius and high productivity set them off by themselves, divorced from the mainstream of the team effort. When this happens, the usual result is

that they drift away and are lost as a resource. They need to be acknowledged.

6. **Recognize potential.** More people have the potential to become high achievers than you would think. In some cases, they need only the right kind of encouragement. Look for those with potential. Ask yourself these questions about each of your people:

(a) Does this employee stand out from the pack and, if so, why?

(b) Is this employee being challenged by his or her present assignment?

(c) How could this employee be challenged further?

(d) What does the employee really want to do?

(e) What should my expectations be?

(f) What boundaries and guidelines does this employee re quire?

7. **Review results frequently.** All too often, high achievers are left on their own, the assumption being that they are self-directed and require neither strokes nor guidance. Not so. High achievers are human, and they enjoy praise, too. And they are members of the team, although they sometimes must be reminded that their individual success is due in part to the opportunity, autonomy, and support they receive from the organization.

*****

Just because high achievers exceed average employees, that does not mean they cannot be inspired to do more.

Thought Provokers

1._____ Do you see yourself as a high achiever?

2._____ Do you feel you have the ability to develop high achievers?

3._____ Do you view your employees' potential realistically?

4._____ Are you alert to ways that a job may be expanded or changed to provide growth opportunities for your employees?

5._____ Are you comfortable pushing an employee beyond his or her apparent limits?

6._____ Do you feel that you provide sufficient challenge to motivate your top achievers?

7._____ Do your employees feel that you recognize the value of their work?

8._____ Do you have higher levels of expectation for those who have greater potential?

9._____ Do you provide the necessary tools to help your employees work in the most efficent, expeditious manner?

10.____ Do you consistently provide more training and information to your people than the company requires?

Chapter 12

OVERCOMING FEAR, ANGER, AND DEFENSIVENESS

People who are strongly inner-directed rarely react in anger.

Overcoming Fear, Anger, and Defensiveness

M arc became a unit manager for Sports Limited in March 1985.

At 6'2" and 195 lbs., he stood out among the dozen women managers with whom he worked. In this women's fitness company, Marc was definitely in the minority. Within weeks, true to his name, he had made his mark--macho, bragging, insensitive, and egotistical. Jill, his supervisor, talked to him on several occasions without success. He continued his act for another three weeks before he was summoned by Cam, Jill's boss, whom you met in chapter 7.

Marc strode into Cam's office, sat down in a chair opposite her desk, and opened with, *"Cam, Jill said you wanted to see me. What's on your mind?"* Cam came quickly to the point, reiterating what Jill had said and adding her own observations. Marc reacted angrily and attempted to justify his position. Cam tried twice more to get through to him without success. Suddenly, she stopped, stood up, walked around the desk, looked down at him and said evenly, *"Marc, it's OK to be afraid."* Marc looked up, stunned. His eyes filled with tears as he managed somewhat awkwardly to get to his feet. In the next few minutes it all poured out. He was indeed afraid of failing, especially in front of women managers. He draped himself over Cam, fully nine inches shorter, and sobbed uncontrollably. He admitted that he'd been terrified on his first day and had tried to cover his fear by bragging, flirting, and joking. As Cam pointed out, however, *"No one bought your act."*

> *...fear is at the root of many people's problems...and it is often masked by other emotions --- anger and defensiveness.*

It would be nice if this story had a happy ending. It didn't. Marc's behavior improved for awhile, but within a few weeks he was back to his old game. Ultimately he was forced to leave. What's the lesson here? What can we learn from Marc's unfortunate experience? There are two points involved.

First, fear is at the root of many people problems, and as in Marc's case, it is often masked by other emotions--anger and defensiveness. Most men have been taught that it is unmanly to show fear or to cry. The emphasis on competition in our culture has furthered this unfortunate misconception. Competition inspires fear, in spite of the myth that *"this country was built on competition."* If myth is true, then it's also true that this country was built on fear. Many highly competitive people run looking over their shoulder. Fear is often deeply submerged in their lives. It's only recently that individuals and companies have been willing to look this monster in the face, deal with fear in themselves and others, and consider cooperation as an alternative to competition.

Second, becoming aware of your fear is only the first step; getting rid of it takes longer, sometimes much longer. Many managers tolerate and overlook fear in their employees, for a variety of reasons--they tell themselves, *"He'll get over it,"* or *"Now is not the time to deal with it,"* or *"Everyone has their bad days."* There may be explanations for their employee's dereliction, but there are no excuses. Fear, left untreated, festers and grows.

Consider the consequences of not confronting fear, anger, or defensiveness in an employee:

- The employee mistakenly concludes that you buy the act and that there are no consequences to repeating the offense.

- Work relationships and productivity suffer.
- In some cases, employees fail on the job and are lost to themselves and the company.

Our extreme emphasis upon competition is based on a fundamental premise: scarcity. We believe that there's not enough to go around, so we think we've got to get ours before everyone else does. Who wouldn't be afraid if there's always a good chance you're going to come out on the short end?

We can't change the world view overnight, but as managers, we can make a difference on a one-to-one basis. Fear seldom serves a useful purpose. It obstructs rather than empowers. Fear is negative energy that nearly always produces negative results. People caught in the fear trap experience a fairly common set of symptoms. They find it difficult to stay focused in the present and become preoccupied with negative past memories or worries about the future. They deny their emotions, adopt compulsive behaviors, and adopt a victim mentality.

Managers are not psychiatrists or counselors. As a manager your role is to manage, to optimize productivity over the long run, and to produce a healthy organization. Because business organizations are objective, task, and responsibility oriented, you cannot always allow people the luxury of growing at their own pace on the job. You cannot tolerate the negative effects of unchecked fear, anger, or defensiveness in yourself or your people. As a manager, you must be on top of the problem. You must be willing to confront these issues with your employees. This is the tough part of being a manager. The nice part is that you <u>can</u> do something about it.

Attitudes and Approaches

L et's look at what the tough/nice approach means in dealing with these emotions. First some general comments, and then we'll examine each separately.

Begin by recognizing that fear, anger, and defensiveness are reactions to a perceived threat. Often troubled employees can't articulate what the threat is, and even if they can, they may choose to conceal their real concern. They may, for example, use anger to mask their fear, or become defensive and uncooperative to prevent you from discovering what's really bugging them. It's your task to dig beneath the shell and find out what's really going on. Regardless of the particular emotion involved, there are three guidelines for dealing with it.

1. **Get beyond your natural tendency to react.** When an employee reacts angrily or defensively, don't compound the problem by reacting yourself. Don't take it personally! Instead ask, What's really going on here? Is the reaction reasonable in terms of the situation (reasonable, not necessarily appropriate or justifiable)? It's a good idea to deal with the underlying issues before tackling the behavior, because solving the problem often results in changed behavior.

2. **Know when to overlook the problem.** If an employee marches into your office and blows up uncontrollably, that may not be the time to deal with it. You may want to discuss the situation later when the employee is more in control. But do deal with it! Just because the employee settles down does not mean that the problem will not arise again. Temporarily overlooking a problem often demands that you set your own feelings aside. When people are fearful or angry, they say and do things that they wouldn't consider in less stressful moments. Listen to your gut, not your ego, and be sure if you elect to confront the problem immediately that you are able to handle it calmly and objectively.

3. **If you have contributed to the problem, be willing to assume responsibility.** You may not want to admit it, but in a surprisingly large number of instances the boss is part of the problem. The manager's own lack of awareness, combined with poor communication and decision-making skills, encourages negative actions in employees. Look hard, and if you have helped create the problem, be willing to admit it and do what is necessary to straighten things out.

Now let's look specifically at each of these emotions and see what you, as a tough/nice manager, can do to help employees overcome their own fear, anger, and defensiveness. Incidentally, although the time frame is generally shorter in work situations than in personal ones, the principles articulated below are the same. They involve objectivity, candor, caring, and a certain amount of courage.

Overcoming Fear

The strongly inner-directed person experiences less fear than others. As a tough/nice manager, you may not feel the fear that your employees do, so your first tendency may be to come down hard. You may tend to neglect the underlying issues and focus only on the behavior. So it's important to understand the nature of fear. Fearful people are to some extent confused about their feelings and unable to take the necessary action to overcome their fear. Fear is a self-defeating emotion, and the tendency to avoid dealing with it is very strong. For the fearful person, there is always the hope that things will get better and the expectation that they won't!

Men and women handle fear differently. From childhood, men have been taught to be competitive, to revere success and deny fear. Women, on the other hand, have been encouraged to be more in touch with their feelings. Recent research shows that women are more disturbed then men by the excessive emphasis on competition and, therefore, are more fearful of success. For many women in the work force, success means increased conflict and pressure to go against their natural inclinations. Consequently, they may be more prone to express fear, anger, and defensiveness when these emotions crop up.

Overcoming Anger

More often than not, anger is concealed fear. Given the option of *"flight or fight,"* many fearful people choose the latter. The most angry employees are often the most fearful ones. This may be hard to see when you are the target. Which brings us to a second point: very often, although the employee's anger may be directed at you, the real object of the anger is someone or something else. You are simply connected, convenient, or in the way. And not infrequently, angry employees are angry at themselves. If you are to help, you must be able to separate the real threat and target from the perceived one.

Should anger be expressed? Is it better to get it off your chest rather than bottling it up? These questions can't be answered with a simple yes or no. The answers depend upon the circumstances. There are, however, some tests you can apply. Ask yourself:

- What is the source of the anger? Why do you (or the employee) feel angry?
- Is the anger justified by the facts?
- How will others be affected by "letting it all out?"
- Are there other ways of handling it than by venting?

Generally, anger must be dealt with. Like the flickering coals of a campfire, anger left alone is apt to smolder and burst into flame, sometimes much later. So the real question is not whether to deal with anger, but when and how to deal with it.

Many managers avoid conflict wherever possible. They ignore, deny, or postpone dealing with tough personnel issues in the hope that the problems will be self-correcting. They fear that if they interfere, their own inadequacies will only make matters worse.

Overcoming Defensiveness

Defensiveness is concealed anger or fear. Whereas fear or anger often pop up suddenly as flash emotions, defensiveness tends to be more deeply rooted and long standing. Consequently, it often requires more time and energy to deal with a defensive person, because the behavioral pattern has developed over a period of time and is apt to be more ingrained.

Steps

Fear, anger, and defensiveness are related, but each has its own characteristics. As a manager, you must decide which you're dealing with. In some situations, all three are involved. You may be able, as Cam was, to sense what is really happening and confront the situation with a simple confirming statement, such as, *"It's OK to be afraid."* In some instances, it may be enough simply to ask, *"What's really bothering you?"* Remember that one of the patterns that attend these emotions is denial, so chances are, that's what you'll get. You can be fairly certain of one thing. Fear is involved in most problem situations. Anger and defensiveness are seldom divorced from fear.

One thing you can do is to begin with the hypothesis that fear is at least an element of the problem and go on from there. Consider the following steps:

Fear

1. **Find out if the employee is fully aware of his or her fear.** Ask questions to determine the employee's level of awareness, for example, *"How do you feel about this?"* or *"Are you worried that you may not be able to handle this situation?"* People often go to great lengths to hide their fear. Their refusal to acknowledge that they are afraid may mean that their fear is mostly at the subconscious level. Your questions, properly phrased and carefully posed, can help them sort out their emotions.

2. **Lead the employee to face the fear.** A simple technique is to have the person write down what bothers him or her. Sometimes several attempts will be required before an accurate statement emerges. Once the fear is defined, however, much of its power is gone. The employee now knows the worst and is ready to consider what can be done about it.

3. **Focus on possible solutions.** Have the employee write down all the options and then discuss them, one by one. Help the person to identify and define the risks and benefits that attend each option. Do a *"best-worst"* scenario by asking, *"What is the worst (best) possible outcome you can imagine?"* Encourage the employee to pick one option that has some prospect of a positive result and then build in provisions for positive feedback. You might, for example, agree to meet again in the future to discuss the employee's progress. With this agreement, you can provide a variety of positive reinforcement messages that indicate you are both aware of the problem, that it isn't insurmountable, and that you are willing to continue to help solve it.

4. **Follow up.** Don't let the matter drop. Make it a point to be approachable. Have an open-door policy. Let the employee know periodically that you are interested. You might want to consider assigning a clear specific task to divert the person's mind and give him or her a sense of accomplishment. Another move is to let the person work with someone who has mastered a similar problem and can

132

serve as an example. Above all, when the employee makes progress, acknowledge it. Build on the strength of his current successes.

5. **Allow the employee to fail.** This is a judgment call that depends on how failure is looked at in your organization. If it is permitted, or encouraged as a means of learning, then allowing someone to fail can help the person to face and deal with fear. But with this permission must go support. Failure can be a powerful learning tool only if it is used carefully.

6. **Finally, you may decide to remove the employee from an impossible situation.** Which option you choose, allowing the person to remain or pulling him or her out, involves a balancing act between your responsibilities to the program and organization and your concern for the individual. Often, there are no clear guidelines. You must do what you are paid to do: make the tough decisions.

Anger

While anger nearly always involves fear, anger is hotter, more obvious. The angry employee gives off signs--terseness, uncooperativeness, white knuckles, and abrupt stiff movements. With practice, you can spot anger much more easily than fear. Once recognized, there are some clear steps you can take:

1. **Prepare yourself.** Don't react to the reaction (anger). Chances are that angry employees are more angry with themselves than at you. In any event, taking it personally only makes the problem more difficult to solve. Focus on the behavior, not the person, and strive to get beneath both to the underlying causes.

2. **Encourage the angry person to express his or her feelings.** If you are suddenly barraged by charges and accusations, pause, wait, and then ask the employee to tell you more (*"Don, I can tell you're upset about this. Can you tell me more about the situation?"*). By handling it this way, you're responding rather than reacting.

3. **Ask questions.** There are several reasons why questions work well at this point. First, they serve to further defuse the anger and encourage the employee to open up. Second, they increase your own

understanding of the situation, although you'll need to go behind the words and listen for the underlying message. That often involves relying on your intuition and then testing it with still more questions. A good thing to remember is that in tense situations the answers often represent statements of feeling rather than fact. The facts can be determined later. What you want to know now is exactly how the person feels. (You might want to refer back to chapters 2 and 3 at this point to sharpen your awareness and communication skills.)

4. Gain further trust by expanding and legitimizing the employee's concern.

5. **Search for alternatives.** Avoid getting boxed in with only one solution. If employees perceive only a single course of action, they may feel that you chose for them and are responsible if things don't work out.

6. **Encourage the employee to select one alternative and then gain agreement that it is the employee who has made the choice.** This places the responsibility for solution where it belongs.

7. **Follow up.** Situations involving anger are often triggered by seemingly unrelated events. It is important to make sure that the problem is solved and not simply transferred to someone else.

Defensiveness

Of the three emotions, defensiveness may be the hardest to break because it represents pent-up emotion and sometimes indicates a pattern of maladaptive behavior. Defensive people have decided that they are right and everyone else is wrong, and are resistant to change.

1. **Prepare yourself as you would with an angry employee.** Don't take it personally, don't react, and above all, don't procrastinate. Anger is often sudden and volatile; defensiveness usually builds up over time. Left untreated, it only gets worse.

2. **Build rapport.** A defensive person doesn't want to open up, so you must find ways of breaking down barriers. Question, expand,

legitimize, and be careful not to say too much. Defensive people will attack if they perceive you as a threat. It may sound trite, but the single emotion you're trying to convey is that you care, and that message will come across only if you really do! Somehow, the employee must begin to trust that you have his or her best interests at heart.

3. **If the employee refuses to open up, risk provoking anger and confront the situation directly even though it might increase the friction still more.** Sometimes this will help dispel the pent up emotions involved. In any case, it is imperative that you keep the confrontation completely impersonal, focused on the issue rather than the person and devoid of anger on your part.

4. **Remember, there is some frustration involved in all defensiveness.** The defensive person doesn't know how to get out of the situation. If you can help the employee see that there are alternatives and that you are sincerely interested in helping find them, you are more likely to be viewed as an ally rather than an enemy.

*****

Confrontation is another management skill that must be learned and one that is critical if you are going to nip potential behavior problems in the bud.

Thought Provokers

1._____ Do you feel that you take charge of your life and create your own opportunities for growth?

2._____ Are you more frequently concerned with what you did wrong than with what you did right?

3._____ Do you confront anger and defensiveness in coworkers and subordinates?

4._____ Is fear a significant motivating force for you?

5._____ Can you express anger directly without accusing or attacking the other person?

6._____ When someone becomes angry with you, do you listen without becoming defensive?

7._____ Can you stick to the subject at hand and avoid introducing irrelevant issues?

8._____ Do you feel hurt when someone becomes angry with you?

9._____ When you are angry, do you become silent and withdrawn?

10. ____ When an employee acts defensively, do you encourage the person to open up in order to uncover the real problem?

11. ____ Do you make excuses to justify your own behavior?

12.____ Do you avoid direct confrontation for fear of losing your temper?

13.____ Do you exaggerate the importance of your own problems in order to gain sympathy?

14.____ Do you blame others for things that go wrong in your life?

Chapter 13

CHANGING PROBLEM BEHAVIOR

A manager's position of authority and power can both be an advantage and a disadvantage. If the manager acts inappropriately, the employee may react in ways that are often termed "problem behavior."

Changing Problem Behavior

Employees don't always perform as expected. On occasion, they can be lazy, uncooperative, and irresponsible and behave in ways that adversely affect their own and others' performance. When this happens, the manager must step in and straighten things out. Unfortunately, many managers are reluctant to intercede, and when they do, their efforts are misguided and ineffective.

Gene Tanner is a case in point. As head of a computer section in a large government agency, Gene managed two dozen programmers and operators. Leah was one of his best people. Until two months ago, she completed her work accurately and on time. Gradually, her work began to slip. She became moody, uncommunicative, and less productive. On several occasions, she came in late or missed work entirely. Gene tried repeatedly to talk with her, but each time he was gently rebuffed. Finally, determined to get things resolved, he ordered Leah to his office. He began by asking her again what was wrong, but Leah maintained her silence. After ten minutes, Gene lost his temper. *"Damn it, Leah,"* he said, *"your work these past few weeks has been going steadily downhill. You've missed four days and come in late several times without a word of explanation. It's obvious that you just don't care."* Leah stared at him across the desk and then, slowly, her eyes began to fill with tears. *"I do care,"* she said, *"but it's clear that you don't!"* With that, she got up and walked out of Gene's office. Fortunately for both of them, one of Leah's coworkers learned of the incident and took it upon himself to talk to Gene. The problem, it seemed, was that Leah had been having severe marital problems. A month ago, her husband had left her for someone else. She felt humiliated and was reluctant to discuss it with anyone.

What went wrong? How could Gene have handled the situation differently? Leah did not make it easy. She refused to open up even after repeated invitations by Gene. But Gene made a mistake many managers make when confronted by a taciturn or recalcitrant employee--he attacked Leah personally and focused only on her overt behavior. As it turned out, her problem was unrelated to the job. Gene never got to the real problem. Instead, he reacted and lost his temper. He failed to realize that Leah's reluctance to communicate was a clear indication that more was involved. Gene should have picked up the signals and, rather than simply questioning her, should have expressed his concern and offered support in a way that would have encouraged her to open up. For example, he might have begun with a statement such as the following: *"Leah, you've been an excellent employee. Until a couple of moths ago, your work has been outstanding. I know you would not let things slip unless there was a good reason. But the fact is, your work has slipped noticeably. As your boss, I have a responsibility to this organization, but I am also concerned about you as a person. Tell me what's going on and how I can help."* A statement such as that has the effect of drawing the employee out and, at the same time, making it clear that the problem behavior cannot be ignored.

> *Unfortunately, in all too many instances, the manager is responsible for the employee's (problem) behavior.*

This brings us to a second point. Problem behavior develops over time. It seldom results from a single incident. The manager has a responsibility to be alert to the early warning signs and to identify and deal with the underlying problem before it reaches a crisis. Unfortunately, in all too many instances, the manager is responsible for the employee's behavior. The manager's actions or inaction causes the employee to react in an unproductive manner. Below are some of the causes, and results (in parentheses), of problem behavior in employees. In all but a few cases, they are factors over which you, the boss, have considerable control.

1. **Disparities between speech and action.** When a manager's practice and preaching are at odds, employees react, usually in a negative way. (resentment, opposition, footdragging)

2. **Lack of clearly articulated goals.** Employees want to know what's expected of them. When they aren't told, they do less than their best. (scattered efforts, mediocre performance)

3. **Unfairness or nepotism.** Most employees expect to be treated fairly. When they feel they are getting the short end, they resent it. (backbiting, gossip, hostility)

4. **Inadequate standards or training.** Employees take their cue from the boss. If standards or training are lacking, the results will show it. (sloppy work habits, poor quality, confusion)

5. **Too much responsibility too soon.** Employees who get in too deep and begin to flounder blame themselves for not being able to make the grade. Often, they become frustrated, fearful, and angry. (poor quality work, mistakes, failure)

6. **Sharing your weaknesses.** Some managers attempt to build rapport by recounting their problems, fears, and shortcomings with their employees. In most cases, that's not what the employee wants to hear. Sharing your weaknesses only increases anxiety. (loss of respect, fear, compulsive behavior)

7. **Conflicting objectives.** When employees sense a disparity between their own and their organization's objectives, their enthusiasm and work suffer. (reduced productivity, increased friction)

8. **Laziness.** There are two kinds: the boss sits back or the employee wants an easy ride. If either is allowed, the eventual outcome is inevitable. (poor work habits, lower productivity)

9. **Intolerance of failure.** Bosses who accept only successes from their people create an environment where caution rather than daring prevails. (half-hearted efforts, limited achievement, less willingness to take risks)

10. **In the wrong job.** Many employees are reluctant to admit that their preference, education, or experience are unsuited to the task they've been assigned. Instead, they become fearful and uncommunicative. (frustration, failure, quitting)

11. **Lack of motivation.** Strong self-motivation follows high self-esteem. It is the manager's task to give a lift where it is needed, to help employees bring out the best in themselves. Many potentially good employees are lost because the manager fails to supply the needed nudge to get them off dead center. (negative attitudes, weak commitment, low productivity)

12. **Excessive ego.** Bosses who throw their weight around or allow their employees to do the same are encouraging weakness in their organization. Ego is a poor substitute for an honest appraisal of one's abilities. (high friction, poor decisionmaking, loss of best people)

13. **Lack of feedback.** From the one-celled amoeba to the most complex human being, feedback constitutes a primary means of learning. Bosses who fail to let their employees regularly know how they're doing deserve what they get. (divided efforts, mediocre results)

14. **Dishonesty.** It always catches up. The manager who is dishonest or tolerates dishonesty in others invites disaster. (loss of trust, increased suspicion, decline in ethical behavior)

15. **Poor work habits.** Managers who come in late and leave early, who leave their desks and work areas cluttered, and who look as though they're wearing the clothes they slept in have no cause to complain when their employees begin to imitate them. (loss of respect, reduced productivity, departure of best people)

16. **Inadequate support.** Employees must be supported. When they're not, they lose confidence and are apt to stop trying. (open resentment, loss of best people)

As a manager, ask yourself: are these characteristic of my organization? Am I partially the cause of the behaviors I criticize in others?

Attitudes and Approaches

Tough/nice managers are sensitive to others' behavior. They detect undercurrents quickly, identify the underlying causes, and act decisively to resolve them. They are alert to the possibility that <u>they</u> may be part of the problem. They establish boundaries at the outset, seek to understand though not necessarily agree with the employee's viewpoint, and explain the "why" of things, up to a point. Once having deliberated, decided, and explained, however, they act to move the employee and the situation off dead center. They treat employees as adults and require that they take responsibility for their actions and for the effects of those actions on others. Finally, they follow up to ensure that the problem is really solved.

Steps

1. **Define the problem behavior for yourself.** How do you see the situation? (At this point, you may find it helpful to talk with others involved rather than the employee.)

2. **Ask yourself how you may have contributed to the problem.** If you have contributed, be willing to acknowledge your mistake and apologize. Once you have apologized, however, don't dwell on your faults; move on.

3. **Before confronting the employee, determine what changes you want to see take place.**

4. **In meeting with the employee, you may find it useful to follow this sequence:**

(a) Tell the person there is a problem. State the problem as you understand it, and explain why it is important that it be resolved.

(b) Gain agreement that you have correctly identified the problem and that the employee understands that it must be resolved.

(c) Ask for solutions. Use open-ended questions, such as, "What are you willing to do to correct this problem?" (In some cases, as with a new employee, you may have to make it clear what you expect.)

(d) Get a commitment that the employee will take the required actions.

(e) Set deadlines. In the case of a repeated problem, you may want to advise the employee of the consequences of failing to take corrective action.

(f) Follow up on the deadlines you have set.

5. **A somewhat special case occurs when the problem behavior involves a personality conflict between two employees.** Then, it is often useful to have each person write down answers to these five questions:

(a) How would you describe the other person? (Focus on your perceptions; use as many adjectives or phrases as you can.)

(b) How does that person make you feel?

(c) Why do you feel the other person behaves the way he or she does? (Here, you are encouraging each person to legitimize, that is to see the situation as the other person sees it.)

(d) In view of your answers to these questions, how do you see your role now? (This question has the effect of shifting the focus to what each person can do to improve the situation. This refocusing alone will often lead to mutually agreeable solutions.)

(e) What conclusions do you draw at this point? (Here you want each person to verbalize the lessons learned as a basis for gaining commitments and setting deadlines.)

*****

Changing problem behavior involves going beyond the *"who"* and *"what"* to the *"why."* What the employee is doing is much less important than why the employee is doing it. The *"why"* provides the key to motivating change.

Thought Provokers

1. _____ Do you encourage your employees to air grievances and frustrations?

2. _____ Before confronting problem behavior in an employee, do you ask yourself if you may have contributed to it?

3. _____ Do you act quickly to deal with problem behavior?

4. _____ Do you acknowledge and apologize for your mistakes?

5. _____ Do you define the outcome you want before confronting the person?

6. _____ Before taking action do you look for the underlying factors that might have caused the behavior?

7. _____ Once the person has accepted responsibility for his or her behavior, do you require a commitment to take the necessary corrective action?

8. _____ In the case of recurring problem behaviors, do you advise the employee of possible consequences?

9. _____ Do you adopt the role of parent when reprimanding an employee?

10. _____ Do you focus on the positive actions that can be taken to influence a change in the behavior?

11. _____ Are you impatient when dealing with an employee who is not articulate or assertive

Chapter 14

EVALUATING EMPLOYEES AND MANAGERS

*Aware managers evaluate daily and hourly.
They know that frequent minor corrections are
more effective than large, sporadic redirection.*

Evaluating Employee and Managers

M anagers who are on top of their job evaluate constantly.

In addition, they conduct periodic formal evaluations as an essential part of the management process. Unfortunately, too many managers are reluctant to evaluate their employees, and when they finally get around to holding formal evaluations, they don't do them well.

Developing a practice of continually evaluating your employees can mean the difference between success and failure, as Steve Lyons discovered. Steve, a management consultant, was asked by the president of a large retail goods company to find out why sales and profits had slipped in several of the stores in the company's eastern region. After a brief meeting with the president, Steve was given a week to do the job and sent out into the field. He began in Baltimore, meeting first with the store manager and then with the various department supervisors. Within three hours, the answers, at least with respect to this store, were obvious. The manager and his supervisors were completely out of touch with their employees. One supervisor reported that she had been on the job nearly two years and had never received a formal evaluation of her work. The principal means of communication seemed to be the weekly staff meetings at which the store manager did all the talking. Two other supervisors observed that the store manager, in his frequent *"inspection rounds,"* was tight-lipped and terse. Lower down, three employees complained that their supervisors seemed to be afraid of the manager, and they felt that no one really cared. It was the same story in two other stores. Within a couple of days, Steve realized that the problem had reached epidemic proportions. Companywide, the pressure to be in touch, to constantly evaluate and guide managers and employees, was missing. The results? High turnover, complaints from customers about poor service and delays, and declining sales and profits.

Many managers subconsciously treat the evaluation process as though it were a conflict situation and avoid it wherever possible. They seem unaware of its many benefits, including:

- Rapport between boss and employee, greater openness in communication

- Mutual respect, particularly when the evaluation is based on jointly determined objectives and measures

- Less fear, as the employee becomes more sure what is expected and how his or her performance is regarded

- Greater awareness, on the boss's part, of the factors that motivate and inspire the employee, and a clearer understanding of the employee's development needs

- Enhanced self-esteem, as the employee begins to feel important and becomes convinced that management cares

Evaluation is a tough process. To evaluate fairly and consistently in a way that yields these benefits demands much of the manager--high awareness, sensitive communication skills, caring, and commitment. Yet, as Steve Lyons can attest, it pays off.

Attitudes and Approaches

Skilled evaluators must be both tough and nice. Tough/nice managers know the importance of regular feedback and discipline themselves and their employees to see that it prevails. They regularly observe and note their employees' performance informally, and they use the formal evaluation as a means of ensuring solid two-way communications with their employees. Their evaluations are based on fair standards and mutually agreed-upon objectives. And finally, they view the process as a way to learn about themselves and their employees.

Steps

It takes practice to become a skilled evaluator. Six steps are involved.

1. **Learn to observe.** Evaluation is a moment-by-moment activity. When one of your employees does something significant, good or bad, note it. Offer praise where it is due and criticism when necessary.

2. **Prepare for the formal evaluation.** Measure performance against objectives, but be attentive to note the existence of new information, or conditions that may make the achievment impossible or inadvisable.

3. **Pick the meeting place carefully.** The evaluation session should always be held in private, never in sight or earshot of other employees. In evaluating a manager, you may want to combine the evaluation with lunch. This is fine if you don't have too many people reporting to you. At a minimum, pick neutral ground, someplace where you are both comfortable. If you anticipate that there may be disagreement, hold the evaluation in a professional setting -- a small conference room or your office.

4. **Decide who should attend.** Normally, only the employee being evaluated would be involved. There are occasions, however, when you might want to invite your supervisor as well. For example, if you're evaluating a manager you are considering for promotion, an additional perspective can be useful.

5. **Orchestrate the session carefully.** State clearly what you want to accomplish and how long you expect the meeting will take, and be sure that the employee understands the standards and objectives being used in the evaluation. Start by asking the employee to summarize

his or her performance during the period. This "you first" approach has two advantages. Where the employee is on target and objective about personal achievements, you can concur and support in a positive manner. It also enables you to sense where the employee is coming from and tailor your remarks accordingly. In the case of poor performance, it gives you an opportunity to help employees see where they have failed to perform.

Use questions wherever possible. Ask things such as, *"Are you satisfied with your performance?" "Where did you exceed your expectations?" "What do you regard as your principal strengths and weaknesses?"* Questions, as we've mentioned before save time and allow you to control the conversation but also allow the employee full expression.

6. **Conclude on a positive note.** You should have accomplished two things at a minimum. First, the employee being rated should clearly understand how you view his or her performance during the past period. Second, you should have reached a mutual agreement as to the employee's objectives during the coming period. Having achieved these ends, there is one final question that clearly sets you apart as a tough/nice manager: *"What support do you need from me?"*

*****

Few employees are self-motivated. Formal and informal evluation can be a strong motivator. Managers who evaluate regularly inspire their people to exceed their limits.

Thought Provokers

1._____ Are you willing to admit your own weaknesses?

2._____ Do you ask for evaluation from your boss?

3._____ Are you sensitive to your employees' opinions of how you perform?

4._____ Do you evaluate your employees regularly?

5._____ Do you allow your employees the freedom to fail?

6._____ Are you fully aware of their strengths and weaknesses?

7._____ Do you understand what motivates each of your employees?

8._____ Do you have fun with your job?

9._____ When you become frustrated or stressed, do you take immediate steps to relieve the pressure?

10. ____ Do you have high standards of integrity?

11.____ Do you treat your staff honestly and fairly?

12.____ Do you have a strong commitment to being successful in your present company?

13.____ Do your employees clearly understand their authority and responsibilities?

14.____ Do you help your employees set concrete, measurable,and mutually agreed-upon goals?

Chapter 15

TERMINATING EMPLOYEES

Most managers do not like to terminate employees, even when there is just cause. Termination, more than any other management process, strikes at the heart of the relationship between the manager and the employee.

Terminating Employees

Why do so many managers have such a hard time terminating an employee? Mike Kent, president of Kent Associates, a graphics design firm in Boulder, Colorado, tells how upsetting the process can be: *"I can't sleep for days before and after I fire someone. It's like a little voice inside of me says that you're guilty of messing up their lives. Even if they're doing a lousy job, I keep thinking maybe I'm responsible for their bad performance."*

For Cam, the female vice-president you met earlier, the crux of the issue seems to revolve around the word *"responsibility"*:

A large part of my job is to help my employees achieve success. I am not an unfeeling type, but the practicality of the situation needs to override any personal feelings I may have for the individual.

It never bothers me to fire an employee for poor performance. The actual termination is the result of a well thought out decision based upon hard evidence and careful reflection. I ask myself and various members of my staff, "Did we do all we could to help this employee?" If I feel that we did, then as far as I can see the employee was not only, not working to his or her potential, but wasn't even up to average performance. The result of their inaction was to take advantage of those around them. The other members of the team had to carry the failing employee's load and divvy up the work with the result that we all suffered.

As far as attitude is concerned, no one likes to work around someone who is negative. I go out of my way during the interview process to tell new employees that a bad attitude is grounds for termination. Our group as a whole is upbeat and works to provide

160

positive energy. So, if we have a person on board who fails to contribute and measure up, termination is a satisfactory answer.

I've learned that good employees look for answers to problems; poor employees bitch and make things worse. A managers has to look at how problem employees affect the organization as a whole. What kind of contributions do they make? If the balance is heavy on the debit side, it can create a ripple effect throughout the organization. Some people are more easily influenced by negatives and bad habits of others. Both managers and employees must set a positive example. We each need to live up to our responsibilities to ourselves, to each other, and to the organization.

If you can identify more easily with Mike's comments than with Cam's, you are not alone. Many managers agonize and procrastinate when it comes to terminating an employee. In delaying, they create problems for themselves, the employee, and others in the organization. In those instances where an employee's performance has been poor enough to justify dismissal, other employees are aware of the problem. When they observe that nothing is being done, they experience a variety of reactions including a loss of respect for the boss, hostility toward the faulting employee, and a general negativity toward the organization.

There are two situations where termination is tough for every manager: company dereliction and economic catastrophe. Let's look at each in turn.

As a manager, you may not be able to force changes in corporate policy or make up for poor past decisions. If you are in a company where deliberate overhiring and subsequent reductions in force are conscious policy--a frequent practice in many companies that operate largely on government contracts--there are several things to keep in mind. First, many of your employees know and accept the practice as a fact of life in the industry and aren't particularly surprised when it happens. The beltway around Washington, D.C., is sprinkled with companies that live off the government and for whom deliberate overhiring is a way of life.

Second, while you may not be able to change the policy, you can be sure that those you hire are aware of it. Many companies are explicit in stating their terms and well known for their practice of contract-only hiring.

Third, to some extent those who sign on just for the job deserve their fate. The fact is that the responsibility for your life is peculiarly your own. It is not that of the organization's or the system's unless that has been specifically agreed to by both parties and reduced to contract. Employers tend to forget this harsh reality when times are good and inducements to join are handed out freely; employees tend to ignore it when times are bad and they need a job. Both sides have obligations. Employees need to ask what the terms of employment are, and employers need to tell them honestly and completely. If there is any doubt, the matter

> *...While you may not be able to change the policy, you can be sure that those you hire are aware of it.*

should be reduced to writing. The employee who asks for these answers and is refused signs on at his own risk.

Finally, as a manager, you have responsibilities to yourself and to your employees. There is no single rule that applies in all cases. There are, however, three questions you might want to ask:

1. Do I feel that this organization owes me a job because of my *"loyalty,"* because of *"all the years I've put in,"* or because of the *"extra effort I give?"* If you do and it does, then you didn't negotiate well in the first place and you must bear part of the blame. Business, and especially employment, is based on negotiation; the outcome, if it is to be a healthy one, should be based on a win/win position. You should be paid for what you do when you do it. If you are not, then the decision to defer part of your rightful income should be acknowledged in writing by both sides. If it is not, then right up front there is an assumption that you are being paid all that you're worth. The same principle applies to your employees.

2. Am I assuming full responsibility for my life? The womb-to-tomb retirement programs so characteristic of the government and many well-meaning paternalistic private employers encourage people to let others (the "system") take responsbility for their lives. When those others fail them, they are distraught. To some extent, we have lost sight of the exploratory pioneer spirit that built this country and that says, in so many words, *"If it's going to be, it's up to me."*

3. Am I encouraging others to assume responsibility for their lives? There is a fine line between making sensible provision for the future and relinquishing your responsibilities with respect to it. With so much pressure in our society to be cared for, it's often an uphill battle to get people to see that the responsibility ultimately is theirs. Yet, that is just what you need to do as a tough/nice manager.

There is one situation where the guidelines are seldom clear and the personal agonizing is even greater: economic catastrophe. The organization is caught in a wave of recession, contraction, downsizing, and declining futures. It is in situations such as these that you, as a boss, may be suddenly called upon to *"pick 20 percent of your people and let them go."* When that happens there aren't any easy answers, but there are some things you might want to consider.

First, there are often guidelines to follow and things you can do to ease the pain somewhat. In organizations where seniority is a negotiated right, for example, the pecking order is pretty much self-evident to everyone, including those who are forced to leave. In many organizations, moreover, there is a variety of options the manager can offer--early retirement, lateral transfer, a lesser position, and out-placement services. Your task as a manager is to understand and apply the guideliens and options as fairly as possible.

Second, when the termination is not the result of poor performance, it is incumbent upon you, to see that the employee leaves with self-esteem intact. The history of a lot of recent blanket firings has been that many terminated employees depart feeling that they are somehow personally responsible for what has happened to them, that they are "guilty" of crimes undefined. Simply talking to the employee and pointing out that this is not the case can help to ease the pain and enable the person to pick up the pieces and go on.

Finally, and this occurs in more organizations than you would think, there is the situation in which both the company and the employee have had ample opportunity to see the writing on the wall. Most of us are awfully good at ignoring what we don't want to hear. Many of the widespread reductions in workforce that have taken place have been in staff positions where the contribution to profit has been questionable. One disgusted cost analyst who fell prey to across-the-board plant reductions commented, in a rare display of candor, *"In a way, I'm glad it's over. I haven't done a damn thing productive in the past six months."*

Attitudes and Approaches

How you approach the task of terminating is critical to how well you accomplish it. Tough/nice managers understand that it is part of the job. They are prepared for it and act on the merits of each case without feeling undue self-recrimination. Like Cam, they have gotten their house in order by the way they treat their people from the day they are first inteviewed, so they have no need to feel guilty. They are realistic in their appraisal of the situation and act to terminate when they determine that other options are inappropriate. They never use the threat of termination to motivate, but are frank to point out the potential ramifications of an employee's failure to perform.

Steps

It is easier to terminate an employee if you have prepared your case and carefully thought out your position beforehand. There are basically six steps involved.

1. **Anticipate problems before they happen.** Identify your marginal people. Build a written record of their failures to perform and your efforts to reach them. Document both informal and formal evaluations and keep copies of pertinent memos.

2. **Be certain termination is the answer.** Ask yourself, *"Is this problem the result of poor supervision, inadequate training, wrong assignments, or mishandling of the employee by the company?"* If any of those applies, you may want to consider other alternatives. How much of the problem is the employee's fault? It's your job as a manager to decide.

3. **Present your position so that the decision is obvious.** If you have prepared properly and have a documented record of valid evaluations, most of your case will have already been made. In a well-managed organization, termination rarely comes as a total surprise.

Your role as a tough/nice manager, often is to confirm what the employee already suspects.

5. **Make it clear that the decision is irrevocable.** A termination session is just that, a meeting to inform the employee of the course of action you have chosen. There is no question of reversing the decision. It is critical that this point be recognized. Managers will sometimes try to soften the blow by being vague about when the actual termination will be effective, or by hinting that radically improved performance might change things. If you have decided that termination is the answer, be firm and get on with it. Don't delay. If you have done your homework properly, your resolve should be solid. And in most instances, it is better to have the terminated employee leave as soon as possible. Keeping him or her around often leads to embarassment and hard feelings.

5. **If you are required to terminate for reasons other than cause, such as companywide layoffs, do it in a manner that leaves the employee's self-esteem intact.** You may want to consider other measures, such as a lateral transfer, a lesser position, part-time work, extended notice, or outplacement assistance.

6. **Today's legal environment presents obstacles to termination.** Be sure that you are current on what you can do and what you cannot.

*****

Failure to terminate an employee whose ethics or performance are below par can have a ripple effect. Managers who keep an employee on under those circumstances send a signal to their people that management cannot be depended upon to make the tough decisions and, just possibly, that sub-par ethics and performance will be tolerated.

Thought Provokers

1._____ Do you have a clear undertanding of your organization's objectives and your employee's roles?

2._____ Do you use termination as a threat to get employees to perform.?

3._____ Do you ever wait too long to terminate an employee?

4._____ Once you have decided to terminate, do you follow through quickly and decisively?

5._____ When terminating an employee, do you find yourself explaining and justifying your decision?

6._____ Would you keep an employee on your staff who is not company oriented and who lacks a strong sense of loyalty?

7._____ When you have warned a problem employee, do you set deadlines and gain agreement as to the changes needed in order for him or her to keep the job?

8._____ Do you follow up on those deadlines?

9._____ Do you often spend too much time working with an employee who has a negative attitude?

10._____ Can you distinguish between behavioral problems and personality traits?

11._____ Do you reprimand employees without becoming angry, defensive, or insulting?

12._____ Do you find that you want success for some people more than they want it for themselves?

Chapter 16

BALANCING SHORT-TERM SUCCESS WITH LONG-TERM PAYOFF

The overwhelming pressure upon the manager is for short-term results. Poor managers succumb. Effective managers find ways to balance short-term results and long-term payoff.

Balancing Short-Term Success and Long-Term Payoff

Jack Steele was Spaulding Construction's lead superintendent. He had a reputation for bringing jobs in below budget and ahead of schedule. Jack's boss, Glen Spaulding, called Jack his *"big gun"*: *"When we have a job with tight budgets and short deadlines, I give it to Jack because I know he'll come through. He has this incredible knack for making it happen."* A heating contractor who worked on several Spaulding jobs saw it somewhat differently: *"Jack is a one tough s.o.b. His only concern is getting the job done as quick and as cheap as possible. He's always looking for ways to cut corners. He fights you to the teeth on extras and if you're behind his schedule, for whatever reason, it's your problem!"*

There were signs, even before that awful day in September 1985. Jack was supervising construction of a ten-storey office building. A day before, they had poured the sixth-floor slab. Suddenly, without warning, the entire slab collapsed, killing one man and injuring several others. Investigation revealed that the forms had been inadequately shored up and that some had been pulled too soon. Glen reacted angrily, *"How could this have happened? You're supposed to be on top of things."* There had been earlier warnings that Glen had chosen to ignore--complaints from an electrical inspector about the wiring, premature peeling of the concrete walks in a condominium development Spaulding had built, and a three-thousand dollar bill for resetting precast concrete floors that had been misaligned. When confronted with these *"minor matters,"* as he called them, Glen replied, *"Look, he's the best man I've got. He makes me money."*

Jack's behavior and Glen's response are symptomatic of an attitude prevalent in all too many companies--the pressure for short-term results at a sacrifice of long-term values. Employees and managers are hired, slotted into positions, given a minimum of training, and told to produce. Many of them become frustrated and bored, and then leave. Turnover rises and management concludes that *"these new people are just not reliable"* and hires more to make up for the attrition. The end result is a mutual cynicism that undermines productivity and trust.

Contrast this attitude with that of the Japanese, who hire the best, define their responsibilities loosely, and train them in virtually every aspect of corporate operations. Specialization, where it occurs, is tempered by a requirement that every manager have a broad and deep understanding of the technology and culture of the organization. In the best Japanese companies--in banking, manufacturing, and electronics--there is a cohesiveness and long-term perspective that is conspicuously absent in many American firms. In all too many American companies, the emphasis is on instant results.

In such situations, it's the managers who suffer. They are the buffer between promise and delivery, unable to change the corporate culture but required to live within it. If they don't produce in the short term, they're not likely to be around for the long term. The plight of one CEO is symbolized in his response to a vice-president who complained about the pressure: *"You just worry about the figures for next quarter. That's what you're paid for. Let me worry about the long term. That's what I'm paid for!"*

Attitudes and Approaches

What can you do to maintain a balance between the two? As a manager, you are paid to achieve results and meet deadlines. Yet you have a responsibility to yourself, your people, and your organization to consider the long-term implications of your actions. This is the hard part. As a tough/nice manager, you must understand your organization's culture and deal with the political realities. You must achieve everything possible and work continually to expand the range of possibilities. Your job demands patience, tact, perseverance, and self-confidence. You must be willing, as the Japanese say,

> *Keeping your eye on the horizon without stumbling over current obstacles requires an intimate knowledge of the terrain.*

to *"nibble around the edges"*--achieve what you can in small increments while sometimes seeming to leave the core untouched. The task is a delicate one.

Steps

Keeping your eye on the horizon without stumbling over current obstacles requires an intimate knowledge of the terrain. It means becoming a student of your organization, its technology, your employees, and yourself. Eight steps are involved.

1. **Understand the culture of your organization.** Study its values, strategies, structure, and communications (formal and informal), and more importantly, learn how to make them work for you.

2. **Know the technology of your industry.** Learn what works and what doesn't. Know how your products, services, and manufacturing processes differ from those of your competitors and why. Understand your industry's development curves and cycles.

3. **Study your employees.** Know their strengths and weaknesses. Learn what motivates and what frightens them. Stand in their shoes and see the situation as they see it, for only in this way can you inspire them to achieve under pressure.

4. **Learn to anticipate problems.** When mistakes occur, accept and learn from them, and then move on. If you're on top of your job and in touch with those who work with you, your perspective will be broader and your timing more certain. As a manager, you are not only captain of the ship; you are navigator and forward watch as well.

5. **Develop a sense of detachment.** You cannot see clearly when you're worried, discouraged, or exhausted. Learn to separate your roles as participant and observer. Take a few minutes each day, and longer each week, to take stock of your job, your problems, and your employees. Picture yourself as an outside observer looking at the situation for the first time.

6. **Train yourself to listen without judging.** Accept information, opinions, and criticism not as true or false but simply as factors to be weighed in making decisions. This willingness to be nonjudgmental is crucial in encouraging others to take the long view.

7. **Set your priorities.** Decide for yourself the appropriate balance between short-term results and long-term payoff. Take time to explain the logic of your decisions to those involved. You may have an intuitive sense of how things should be, but others will want to know how you arrived at your conclusions. Let them know so they can support you.

8. **Report up from a position of strength.** Remember, your boss faces similar pressures. Know the facts and details of your unit's performance and be able to relate them to specified objectives. When you sit down with your boss, be prepared:

(a) Anticipate your boss's questions. Most managers are fairly predictable. If you study your boss, you'll learn to sense in advance what's on his or her mind.

(b) Deal with disparities, objections, and criticisms directly. If you expect that your boss will nail you on an issue, bring it up first and dispose of it. Your boss will appreciate your thoroughness and attention to detail.

(c) Get your boss's commitment. You report not only to give information, but to show that you are in control of the situation and your organization. Often, all you have to do in order to gain your boss's commitment is to ask for it by posing questions such as, *"Do you agree that the actions we've discussed should put us back on target?"* Properly phrased questions, once you have set the stage, enable you to obtain your boss's commitment without putting him or her on the spot.

*****

Individual managers are held responsible for short-term success. Long-term payoff is somehow regarded as a collective responsibility, with the result that no one is responsible.

Thought Provokers

1. _____ Are you fully aware of your organization's culture its values, strategies, structure, and communications?

2. _____ Do your employees understand the differences between the short-term objectives and long-term goals toward which they are working?

3. _____ Do you report up from a position of strength?

4. _____ When your boss raises objections or criticisms, do you deal with them directly?

5. _____ Do you gain commitment from your boss?

6. _____ Do you make demands in proportion to the results you expect?

7. _____ Do you know how your product or service differs from that of your competitors?

8. _____ Do you frequently have problems meeting deadlines?

9. _____ Do you time-manage your employees?

10. _____ Do you plan for your employees to experience short- term successes?

11. _____ Do they experience long-term payoffs as well?

12. _____ Does your company consistently stick with its long- range goals?

Chapter 17

TURNING A FAILING OPERATION AROUND

The turnaround specialist is a troubleshooter
brought in to assess the situation quickly,
develop solutions, and act accordingly. Under these
circumstances, the greatest contributions are objectivity
and toughness.

Turning a Failing Operation Around

Not every management assignment begins happily. Disasters happen, and when they do, the best managers are called to the rescue with few ground rules to guide them. They are thrown into situations where the full extent of the damage is often unknown and where the problems typically have a long, clouded history. Apprehension is high, feelings raw, and memories often unclear. Turnaround managers are left on their own with only vague assurance that they will have the support they need.

If you've been asked to step in and pick up the pieces of a failing operation, make no mistake: you will be facing one of the most challenging assignments of your career. You will be coming into the middle of the play with only the most sketchy script as to what has gone on before. You face great opportunity and great risk. You are expected to succeed where others have failed. If you accept the challenge (and in many cases, you have no choice, for the request is really a demand), you should be aware of the facts that attend most turnaround situations, namely:

- The problems may be more obvious because they've reached crisis proportions, but they are also more difficult to fix. The easy solutions have been tried and have failed.

- Fear, frustration, and negativity are high, and confidence, enthusiasm, and optimism are low.

- Depending on how soon you are called in, the bulk of the good people may have become discouraged and left, and you may have to fire many of those who remain.

- The "problem" you've been asked to fix usually turns out to be a series of problems that have resulted from the original one. For example, poor product quality (an internal problem) may have already resulted in the loss of customer confidence (an external problem). You may be able to solve the quality problem fairly quickly, but the lost confidence can be regained only over time. Chrysler and Continental Airlines can attest to this.

Perhaps the worst situation to contemplate, but one that is realistic in today's large bureaucratic organizations, is that the boss who brought you in may be the problem! In that case, you may find that the situation ca't be rectified and that you are to be the scapegoat.

All of this points to one thing: you owe it to yourself to ask some tough questions before you become involved and make commitments you cannot keep.

- Is the problem solvable in a manner short of scrapping the whole operation? Has it been allowed to go on too long?

- Is the problem, as defined, the real problem and the entire problem? (The answer to this question is critical in helping you define the authority, time, and resources you will require to fix things.)

- What is the planned or required time frame for the turnaround, and what are the limits of your authority? What support can you expect?

- Finally, are you expected to stay with the operation after the turnaround has been accomplished, or can you expect to be pulled out? (Which outcome is intended can have a significant impact on how you go about your task.)

Even with awareness of the facts, you should know that you are in a situation that requires a special sensitivity. A solid knowledge of the technology of the industry is essential. In turnaround situations, you don't have time to learn the ropes and you can't afford to trust others to guide you. In a real sense, you're on your own, highly visible and carefully observed. Beyond this initial familiarization, the manner in which you approach the task can be critical.

Attitudes and Approaches

Tough/nice managers confronted with a turnaround situation have an edge over their colleagues. They address the problem in terms of "what" rather than *"who."* They are less concerned with who is at fault than with what is needed to correct the situation. That disposition shows through as those involved begin to sense that they are seeking positive solutions rather than attempting to punish wrongdoers.

It is perhaps in the stressful conditions of the turnaround situation that the inner qualities of tough/nice managers are most apparent. Their inner-directedness and balance are reflected in the purposeful poise they exude. Similarly, their ability to remain flexible and move ahead confidently demonstrates their own commitment and inspires dedication in others.

Steps

As a turnaround specialist, you will be the center of attention. Your success will depend upon your preparation, the speed and assurance with which you act, and the consistency of your approach and follow-through. Nine steps are involved.

1. **Be certain your assignment and authority are clear and explicit.** Is your job to rejuvenate the organization or to dismantle it? Does your boss understand the problem? What support can you expect? What are the limits of your authority? What are the objectives and time frames for which you are responsible? Will you have the resources required to do the job? Get answers to these questions before you move.

2. Do your own damage assessment. Don't accept anyone's word about what has happened, how bad it is, or what can be done about it. In disaster situations, everyone runs for cover. No one is sure of what's going on and everybody is suspicious. Expect that the information you get will be biased, incomplete, and sometimes unwillingly shared. Don't be surprised. It's understandable and normal. Ask questions and confirm the answers you get.

3. Define your boundaries early. Since you're facing a crisis situation, there isn't time for everyone to become accustomed to your management style. Those affected need assurance, clarification, and direction as soon as possible. Some will already have reached a panic state. To get them moving, you must be explicit about how you plan to go about the task and what they can do to help.

4. Initiate action, set objectives, and establish deadlines. This provides a sense of momentum and gives people confidence that they are becoming part of the solution.

5. Provide regular feedback. Where possible, your emphasis should be positive. There will be hard decisions to make -- demotions, transfers, and terminations. Make them when necessary, and where possible, deal only with the people who are directly involved. Inform others in a way that adds perspective to your decisions -- your reasons for making them and the positive results you expect.

6. Know when to cut your losses. In any disaster situation, some people and operations are simply not salvageable. Remember your original objectives. Realize why you are there: because you bring incisiveness, experience, fairness, and needed toughness to a difficult situation. Maintaining a sense of balance when really hard decisions are required isn't easy, but it's what you're paid to do. The business must be profitable to survive. Every employee realizes that. So, profit is an essential part of the survival equation. When an individual or an operation must be terminated, do it fairly and decisively, as a way of achieving the greatest good for the greatest number within the framework of your stated objectives.

7. Give credit where credit is due. The word *"turnaround"* implies that people, processes, policies, and practices are changed for the better. When people do change, recognize their efforts in tangible ways. Let them know they are contributing. It pays off handsomely in dedication and loyalty.

8. **Review what has been accomplished.** Most troubled operations afford lessons applicable to other operations. It is important to realize what you have gone through, internalize what you have learned, and communicate the lessons to others who can benefit.

9. **Redefine your objectives and goals.** A revitalized operation looks different. Your initial concern was to solve the most critical problems and get the operation moving again. Now you must help people focus their energies in a positive direction. You do this by providing both short-term and long-term perspectives with which they can identify.

*****

Few managers are equipped to handle turnaround situations, in which invariably the problems are harder, the risks greater, and the rewards less certain. It requires a special kind of person to face the challenges of a hostile atmosphere and still maintain self-confidence.

Thought Provokers

1. _____ Would you feel comfortable taking on a turnaround situation?

2. _____ Are you willing to ask tough questions in order to get to the heart of the problem, define your authority, and learn what is expected of you?

3. _____ Can you get up to your elbows in detail and still maintain the larger perspective?

4. _____ Are you comfortable moving into a situation that involves fear, suspicion, and open hostility?

5. _____ Are you confident of your ability to distinguish between legitimate concern and biased criticism?

6. _____ Do you move into new situations quickly, establish your boundaries clearly, and require that those involved get moving?

7. _____ Do you give regular and timely feedback to those who have a need to know?

8. _____ Are you experienced in cutting your losses?

9. _____ Are you confident of your ability to make decisions in the face of limited information and time?

10. _____ Can you give credit where it is due without focusing on yourself?

Chapter 18

CONDUCTING MEETINGS

In organizations where there is open communication, formal meetings are kept at a minimum. Those that are held are more productive and waste less of the manager's time.

Conducting Meetings

M onday morning management meetings at Bonnet Chemical were legendary. Lou Bonnet, president, CEO, and part-time thespian, was known for his colorful meeting style. His lengthy openers were spiced with funny stories, one-liners, and good-natured ribbing. Lou ran the meetings in a relaxed, easy manner that put everyone at ease. Then hard times hit Bonnet. Sales and profits dropped by more than a third in less than a year. The board directed Lou to review every department and operation in the company with a minimum initial target of a 20 percent reduction in costs. Nothing was immune to scrutiny.

The Monday after the board's action, Lou chaired his first humorless meeting. Vice-presidents and department heads were told to develop new sharply reduced budgets and staffing plans. Each member of the management committee was directed to analyze personal time expenditures for the previous month and to identify areas in which significant time had been wasted. The committee met again the next week, budgets and analyses in hand. And there, at the top of nearly everyone's list of wasted moments, was a single subject--meetings. Not just the Monday morning meetings but a string of others that followed Lou's regular get-together style. Vice-presidents reported they had been spending more than 50 percent of their time in meetings. For the department heads, the situation was even worse--nearly 75 percent. Meetings at Bonnet had become a habit, convenient, comfortable, and entertaining, but terribly wasteful in terms of the time they consumed.

Bonnet's story is not unique. Many companies have discovered that hard times sharpen their vision and expose the fact that many meetings are not worth the time they consume. All too many are colossal time-wasters, poorly conceived, and even more poorly executed.

Communication is a major executive function in today's information society. Most executives and managers spend the majority of their time communicating. Meetings are only one often very expensive means. Studies of Bonnet and other companies reveal why most meetings cost more than they're worth. Some of the more common reasons are:

- Lack of concrete objectives.
- Inadequate planning and preparation.
- Poor meeting management.
- Confusion between habit and ritual.
- Including the wrong people, or too many people.
- Failure to capitalize on the individual differences of those attending.
- Monologues by the chair, speeches and interruptions by others.
- Poor scheduling, such as after lunch *"naptime"* meetings.
- Inappropriate physical arrangements.
- Slick versus substantive presentations
- Poor cost/benefit ratios, especially when time costs are calculated.
- Lack of follow-up

Good meetings are like a symphony; bad meetings are more like a sock hop. Good meetings are orchestrated; they don't just happen, as George Lundberg discovered recently. George, vice-president for production for a New England electronics firm, flew to Japan to arrange for the production of several electronics subassemblies. He was accompanied by the purchasing and engineering vice-presidents and given two weeks to do the job. Within a week, George was frantic: *"What are these people trying to do?"* he asked an American businessman who had lived in Japan for ten years. *"They schedule a meeting at eight in the morning and they don't arrive till ten. They ask questions, nod their heads, and deliberate for hours, but they don't make decisions!"* His friend listened as George vented his frustration at *"being had"* and then replied, *"George, my friend, you've just been exposed to the Japanese style of conducting meetings. For these people, the manner in which things are done is critical. Nuance is as important as substance. Pace and timing rather than confrontation are used to surface and resolve key points in a negotiation. You'll find that most Japanese negotiations refuse to be hurried. Their principal strategy is purposeful indirectness."*

Attitudes and Approaches

We have observed that most meetings are not worth the time they consume. Certainly George Lundberg felt that much of the time he spent negotiating with the Japanese was not well spent. George's experience, however, reveals an important point about the meeting process: it's not how much time is spent but how well it is spent that counts. Many managers use meetings indiscriminately, much as a novice golfer might attempt to use an eight iron in all situations. Running a good meeting is an art that requires careful planning and attention to nuance. The skilled meeting planner can accomplish much.

> *Communication is a major executive function in today's information society.*

Tough/nice managers use meetings well. They are sensitive to strategic aspects and are equally effective as orchestrator and conductor. They decide in advance what is to be achieved and plan carefully. They select participants in terms of how each can contribute and benefit, and pay close attention to agenda and clock. Their meetings start and end promptly and are constructive and challenging. Participants feel that their time has been well spent.

Steps

Running an effective meeting demands careful preplanning, tact, and communicative skill. Poorly run meetings reflect adversely on your abilities as a manager. You cannot ignore any aspect of the process. There are fourteen steps involved in conducting effective meetings:

1. **Define your objectives.** Too many meetings are held routinely and without regard for what they are to achieve. Is your purpose to inform, instruct, gain agreement, soothe hurt feelings, or reach a decision? Depending on your style, you may use meetings to build cohesiveness within your management team. If you do, be sure that you distinguish between deliberate ritual and habit. The every Monday morning meeting can be good or bad, depending upon how clearly you define your objectives and how adept you are as a conductor.

2. **Decide if the meeting is really necessary.** Can you achieve your objectives in another way? Would a memo or an informal gathering of fewer people work just as well? Will the meeting be worth the costs of preparation and the people-time involved?

3. **Select an appropriate strategy.** If directness is your style, there's nothing wrong with calling a meeting to *"tell it like it is"* if you don't squelch all the feedback. If your objective is consensus and teamwork, however, you may want to temper your style in order to encourage more openness.

4. **Determine who should attend and why.** Think how each person can contribute and benefit. Do you want to gain agreement or surface differences? Who you invite can make a difference in the outcome. Sometimes you may invite people who you know will disagree and dispute, especially if you feel there has not been an adequate airing of the issues involved.

5. **Pick the place and time.** Consider both turf and comfort. Taking people away from the office helps get their attention and lets them know that the meeting is important. On the other hand, meetings off premises are more expensive unless they can be combined with dining or commuting. Some managers have a practice, for example, of holding breakfast meetings before work at a nearby restaurant.

6. **Give adequate notice.** Develop and distribute the agenda in advance. If others are to make presentations, be sure that you give them adequate time to prepare.

7. **Determine what information can be distributed prior to the meeting.** Most people read faster than they speak. The written word often is preferable to oral presentaion, especially if you want participants to digest the information before coming to the meeting. If you distribute material separately from the agenda, refer to the specific agenda item to which it applies.

8. **Follow up with a reminder.** Busy people often forget even written appointments. Avoid embarrassment. Have your secretary call the day before.

9. **Check the logistics.** Even if you've used the room many times before, check and make sure that seating, lights, equipment, and temperature are correct. Things have a way of going wrong at the last minute, so a spot check is always useful.

10. **Start promptly.** First time around, warn those attending that you intend to begin on time. From then on, do it. This shows that you respect others' time and lets everyone know that the meeting is important.

11. **Manage the meeting.** Decide beforehand how you want the meeting to go. If you want to reach a decision, for example, keep the focus on that objective. Be firm about the ground rules. Don't tolerate long monologues (yours or anybody else's), interruptions, or pointless rambling. Use questions to bring out important points and to reconcile differences. Make use of individual differences. For example, a negative person can be used very effectively to surface

aspects of issues that advocates may want to ignore. Learn when not to make the decision. Careful meeting management can result in consensus that does the job for you!

12. **Summarize.** Review you original objectives. Have you attained them? If not, why? Recap the discussion in a way that restates the objectives and let's everyone know the extent to which they have been achieved.

13. **End on time.** This lets those attending know that you value their time. If you must run over, ask permission for the additional time needed. And don't forget to thank everyone for coming. It's common courtesy and it lets them know you care.

14. **Follow up.** Evaluate the results. Did you accomplish your objectives? Did others perform as agreed? What needs to be done as a result of the meeting? Make a list of the actions to be taken and follow through to see that they are completed on time. Finally, distribute minutes of the meeting within twenty-four hours. Your minutes should state clearly any actions to be completed and deadlines for their accomplishment. People appreciate the follow-up. It makes them look better as well.

*****

You can gauge a manager by the way he or she conducts meetings. Meetings reveal the manager's style for all to see.

Thought Provokers

1._____ Do you spend too much time in meetings?

2._____ Do you plan your meetings in advance?

3._____ Do you give others adequate notice if they are to prepare materials for a meeting?

4._____ Do you make it a point to begin and end your meetings on time?

5._____ Do you do most of the talking when conducting a meeting?

6._____ Do you preplan questions for discussion?

7._____ Do you brainstorm to surface new ideas?

8._____ Do you control the meeting and minimize unnecessary chatter?

9._____ Do you ask for feedback on the effectiveness of your meetings?

10._____ Are you aware of the values of having minority and negative views represented?

11._____ Are you alert to notice when your meeting starts to drag?

12._____ Do you end your meetings by summarizing and thanking participants for their attendance?

13._____ Do you keep track of your meeting successes and failures?

Chapter 19

BECOMING A TOUGH/NICE MANAGER

Being both tough and nice is difficult. It's easier to be one or the other. The problem is, it takes both to be an effective manager.

Becoming a Tough/Nice Manager

Tough/nice managers are atypical. They comprise something less than one-fifth of the management population. Like Thoreau, they march to a different drummer and the beat is largely their own. They are strongly inner-directed, inwardly balanced, and flexible. They choose their own path and manage to stay on course regardless of setbacks and detours. They are powerful, less because of the externals of their life than because of their own centeredness. They are committed "100 per cent full on," but to approaches and directions uniquely their own. Finally, they are high achievers, people who operate at the upper edge of their abilities and who, through change and growth, constantly strive to expand their limits.

Becoming anything worthwhile demands desire, dedication, and discipline. You've got to <u>want</u> to become a tough/nice manager. That's the first step. Before you decide, you should consider the disadvantages. It's not all fun and games.

Disadvantages of Being a Tough/Nice Manager

People expect more of you. Chances are you're different from other managers who preceded you. To begin with, you're less predictable, a mix of opposites--tough and nice, bold and cautious, caring and demanding. That makes you unusual, perhaps a bit mysterious, and somehow more capable in others' eyes. Maybe it's your inner-directedness, but people come to rely on you for answers they don't get from more traditional thinkers.

You expect more of yourself. When you begin to discover your full capabilities, it's natural to become dissatisfied with where you are. There is so much more to learn, more things to do, more mountains to climb. Before you know it, you're demanding more of yourself and getting it.

You expect more of others. When everyone adheres to a single standard, individual differences are minimized. If one person moves ahead, comparisons are inevitable. When you leave the pack, it's amazing how much more distance you can cover. In such situations, it's hard not to become more demanding. The only saving grace is that you tend to make positive demands, because you have a greater sense of potential, your own and others'.

Distinctions between work and play become blurred. Before you became a tough/nice manager, it was nice when five o'clock rolled around and you could leave it all behind. Then, somewhere along the way, you made some decisions. Maybe you changed jobs or moved into an organization where you felt more committed. Regardless of the specifics, you found a way to make work seem more like play. Now you're stuck. Five o'clock doesn't have the significance it once had, and you occasionally find yourself working far into the night. In this blurring of boundaries, you've become more "aligned," that is, you're able to focus your energies more intently for longer periods of time, and you enjoy it!

It's harder to give loyalty. Remember how proud you felt when you got that first big promotion? It was easier then to be loyal to the organization that gave you the chance. Now, there's an inner need to be loyal to yourself, to follow your own path wherever it leads. Somewhere between then and now, loyalty to yourself outdistanced loyalty to organization.

Quality of life becomes more important. The problem with demanding more of yourself is that you also want more out of life --

quality rather than quantity. You turn down a promotion/transfer to New York in order to get an advanced degree, or chuck a job in a Fortune 500 company for a position in a smaller firm where you can make an impact. Moments become precious.

People take more of your time. When things were simpler, people weren't so important. Facts were all that mattered and issues were clear cut. You didn't have to be concerned with people's personal problems. As long as they came to work on time and did their job, things were fine. It's no longer that simple. There are more people issues, and the solutions are more complex.

Others misjudge you. Someone once observed that you can separate seasoned managers from novices simply by how much they talk. As a tough/nice manager, you've learned the value of listening. When you respond to another's questions or challenge, your reply is apt to be more thoughtful, even tentative. You've discovered the virtue of indefiniteness and are less willing to volunteer solutions to others. Unfortunately, those who prefer explicit direction may misinterpret your actions and regard you as indecisive or uncaring.

More often than not, you have to go it alone. When the stakes are high and deadlines short, you can't always wait for consensus. Sometimes you must act, decide before others fully understand, and take responsibility for the consequences.

Others may be threatened. Not everyone welcomes your company. Some will be intimidated by your awareness, your willingness to communicate directly and openly, and your capacity for moving quickly to the crux of the problem. You may be feared or attacked because you are capable.

You may outgrow your friends. No two people grow in identical ways. Some prefer comfort to challenge, and stability to change. For them growth is secondary to happiness. As a tough/nice manager, your priorities are different. Your heightened self-expectations cause you to put growth first and to experience a constructive restlessness that sometimes separates you from your peers. Excellence has its costs, one of which is that you may leave some of your friends behind as your attitudes and patterns change.

You may be accused of being lucky. Often, one's intuition is not obvious to others. As a tough/nice manager, your intuitive grasp may be much stronger than that of your colleagues. When you make decisions or take action without explaining yourself, people are likely to attribute the results to luck. Even when you hit consistently, they'll be inclined to call it chance and accuse you of being inconsistent or unpredictable. Having strong intuition is just another reason why you must be willing to go it alone.

Not everyone will want to hire you. Mediocre organizations are easily intimidated by outstanding performers. As a tough/nice manager, you've set high standards for yourself and for those who employ you. Only the best employers welcome the candor displayed by an applicant for the position of research director in a medium-sized electronics firm. When asked what kinds of people he preferred to work with, he replied: *"I want the people I associate with to be at least as bright as I am."* He got the job! As a tough/nice manager, you're still in the minority, and so are the companies who will be comfortable with your management style.

Deciding To Go For It

Look again at those disadvantages. Do you detect a common thread? Well, there is one and it's this: all of the negatives to becoming a tough/nice manager can be positive influences that force you to grow. Growth requires dedication, commitment, and a willingness to sacrifice some things in order to gain others.

It's hard to be fully committed when your energies are divided. A commitment to excellence is just that, being outstanding in all areas of your life in order to grow in all areas. If you really want to grow, it's hard to accept mediocrity in any part of your life. There is always that inner demand to be better. People who accept this fact invariably find that outstanding performance is contagious. It spills over into everything and leads to an awareness that everything is connected in some inexplicable way.

We've talked about becoming a tough/nice manager as though it were a single achievement, like becoming a sergeant. Actually it's a continuing process of becoming aware of qualities within yourself and of developing the skills, attitudes, and practices involved. And, as you'll see in just a moment, there are several ways to do it. But, before you begin, there's a preliminary step involved.

Conducting your own self-assessment. We've found three techniques that are particularly useful in assessing where you are now. The first two are fairly easy to accomplish. The last is a bit more difficult to arrange.

Begin by asking yourself several questions. Your answers will reveal the extent to which you recognize tough/nice qualities in yourself:

- When a problem or crisis arises, do I first look within myself for solutions?

- Do I maintain a sense of balance in my life between work and play, fun and seriousness? Am I comfortable with opposites in my character?

- Do I adapt easily to sudden changes and unforeseen circumstances?

- Am I in control of my life? When a crisis occurs, do I avoid asking, "Why did this happen?" and look immediately for a solution?

- Am I committed, "100 per cent full on" in what I'm doing now?

Your answers will help you determine the extent to which you are inner-directed, balanced, flexible, powerful, and committed.

You'll recall that we said that preference rather than ability determines how successful you will be in in the longrun. A second step, therefore, is to examine your preferences -- how you choose to deal with the world around you. An excellent technique for doing this is the Myers-Briggs Type Indicator. This device measures your preferences with respect to perceiving and judging, that is, the extent to which you approach the world primarily through the five senses or intuition, and whether your judgments are based primarily on logic or feelings. Understanding your preferences in these areas is important, for your preferences determine how you approach problems, your job, and others. Understanding your *"type,"* as it is called in Myers-Briggs terminology, enables you to relate more effectively to those who think differently than you do.

Finally, and this is harder to do, it's useful to discover how others view you. We use a formalized assessment technique that allows managers to compare their self-perceptions against the perceptions of colleagues and friends. While some managers see themselves pretty much as others see them, this is not usually the case. The disparity, moreover, increases as you get higher up the management ladder. When you think about it, this isn't really surprising. The higher you rise in an organization, the less willing people will be to point out your faults. They're more apt to tell you what they think you want to hear. Having an assessment done on yourself can be tough. You may learn things you don't want to know. The point is, if you're going to succeed as a tough/nice manager, it's important that you project the real you. Viewed in this way, disparities are simply opportunities to develop greater awareness and to learn to communicate more effectively.

Going For It

If you decide you want to become a tough/nice manager, there are several ways to go about it. We separated the task chapters into *"Attitudes and Approaches"* and *"Steps."* Depending on your type (Myers-Briggs), you may feel that one or the other is more useful. For example, if you're highly intuitive, you might find yourself rereading chapter 1 and concentrating on the attitudes and approaches sections in the task chapters. If, on the other hand, you're a high *"sensing"* type, you may want to begin by following the steps presented in each chapter. Either way works. Changes in attitude will help you become more receptive to different ways of doing things. Conversely, simply <u>doing</u> things differently, following the steps, will cause changes in attitude. You can even begin by working to increase your skills in awareness, communication, and problem solving. Skills mastery in these areas inevitably leads to changed attitudes and practices.

Whichever option you choose, there are four steps involved. Don't omit any of them.

1. **Develop a plan.** Simply resolving to do better won't make it. It is imperative to have some idea of where you want to go or you'll never get there. Your plan, whether it be a formal document or a sheaf of handwritten notes, should consist of four parts:

Goals. Things you want to achieve in the next one to ten years or longer. You can have goals in several areas--professional, financial, educational, family, social, and personal. They should be brief, concise, and few in number. You may have one or two goals in each of the above categories, but avoid having more or you won't achieve them. Your energies will be divided.

Objectives. Things you plan to achieve in less than a year or less. Typically, you'll have more objectives than goals, because your objectives define events that must occur before your goals can be achieved. In this area as well, it's important to avoid having too many.

Tasks. A task is something you must accomplish in order to achieve an objective. Tasks answer the *"what"* questions, for example *"What must take place in order for me to achieve this objective?"*

Steps. The specific actions you must take in order to complete each task. Steps answer the *"how"* questions regarding objectives.

We said that the tough/nice manager must master three key skills. Actually, there's a fourth. It's the process of planning and execution that we call *"work/life management."* Here's an example of a work/life plan, illustrated in terms of a single goal. In a complete plan, of course, you would have several goals. For purposes of illustration, let's consider how the plan develops from just one goal:

Goal: Become self-employed within five years.

Objectives: (1) Position myself so as to be able to span the transition period when income is reduced. (2) Determine the industry and product or service I want to be in.

Tasks: (pertaining to objective #1): (1) Define minimum and optimum cash needs for each year during the learning period. (2) Explore alternatives for earning more and spending less.

Steps: (pertaining to task #1): (1) Analyze expenditures for the past three years. (2) Forecast bare-bones outlays for the coming period (education, housing, transportation). (3) List items and amounts of planned discretionary spending.

Your work/life plan is shaped like a pyramid in that the detail increases as you move down through the plan. You may have two or three objectives for a single goal, several tasks for each objective, and several steps for each task. You move from general goals to specific steps, each connected from bottom to top.

2. **Take action.** Plans that aren't implemented gather dust. It's important that you take positive, concerted action. Begin with the steps and work toward your objectives. Your achievement is measured by the extent to which you complete the steps and so accomplish your objectives. You can avoid the frustration of wondering if it will ever happen by putting most of your effort on things you can do now or in the immediate future.

3. **Visualize your achievements.** Too many people write impressive plans and achieve only limited results. What is it that prevents them from achieving what they've set out to do? Often it's a failure to visualize, to *"feel"* the ultimate result. If you really want to achieve your objectives and goals, you must be able to experience them as having already happened. This process of seeing your goals as already attained aligns your energies and prepares you to adapt to changing conditions while still not losing your overall vision. If you think this sounds a bit too touchy-feely, consider this: the Soviets were able to improve the performance of their Olympic athletes significantly by having them visualize the act of performing perfectly (according to plan) as part of their normal training routines. Visualization is used extensively in many areas of sports today, with extraordinary results.

4. **Model, don't mentor.** The problem with mentors is that, inevitably, they fail to meet our expectations and we outgrow them. Parents turn out to be less than perfect. Professors appear more provincial when we meet them ten years later. Favorite bosses make mistakes, sometimes huge ones. The point is, model the behavior and not the personality. As one manager put it, *"I'll learn from the devil,*

if he has something to teach." We learn best by modeling, metaphor, trial and error. Don't imitate someone else's style. Develop your own.

4. **Be willing to dump your plan.** Mike Kent, whom you met in chapter 15, put planning in an especially clear perspective when he remarked, *"I revise my five-year plan every week."* After two decades of hype and nonsense regarding long-range planning, companies are becoming aware that the value of planning has little to do with the accuracy of the forecast. Plans are a most useful a means of gaining perspective and communicating with others who are involved. As your vision improves, goals set earlier may prove to be unworkable. Don't be afraid to change or even discard them if need be. Remember, flexibility is a key quality of the tough/nice manager.

*****

Tough/Nice is neither a technique to be mastered nor a style to be emulated. It is a result of the inner qualities that make up the person.

THE DELTA GROUP

Everyone has the potential to become a high achiever. We are committed to helping individuals discover and utilize their full potential. We do this through a series of workshops that focus on making your career and life work better. While these workshops cover a variety of topics relating to management development and personal growth, they all share certain common characteristics. They are:

- **Intense.** Those with whom we have had the privilege of working describe their experience as *"forceful"*, *"dynamic"* and *"focused"*.

- **Interactive.** Lecture is held to an absolute minimum in favor of full and active participation.

- **Team Taught.** We work together as facilitators offering both breadth and differences in views and approach.

- **Experiential.** Our programs are based on our own experience in a variety of fields and industries rather than on reportorial dexterity.

- **Integrated.** We approach individual growth from two perspectives simultaneously: the inner aspects of self motivation, direction, and significance; and the outer world of techniques and practices.

- **Individually centered**. We tend to work with smaller groups, typically less than twenty-five people, so that we can address each individual's concerns thoughtfully and sensitively.

Illustrative Programs

We do a variety of programs for companies, governement agencies, and private groups. By way of illustration, three of our more popular programs are:

- **Becoming a High Achiever.** A three-day intensive workshop limited to a maximum of twenty-four participants, available to companies and other organizations. This program involves significant pre-session homework and pre-session analysis on our part approximating one and a half hours per participant.

- **Making Your Life & Career Work.** Taught at the University of Colorado as a ten week course and also available as a three-day intensive workshop for groups of fifteen or more.

- **Managing the Change Process.** A two-day workshop which presents an organized approach to accomplishing organizational and individual change.

If you are interested in a workshop for your organization or group, you may contact us care of The Delta Group, 245 Ponderosa Way, Box 40 Evergreen, Colorado 80439. If you would prefer, you may call us at 303/674-9850. For your convenience, a detachable request form is included following this page.

REQUEST FOR WORKSHOP INFORMATION

The Delta Group
245 Ponderosa Way
Box 40
Evergreen, Colorado 80439
(303) 674-9850

Dear Candy and Shale,

I've read your book, *Tough/Nice,* and am interested in learning more about your workshops. Would you please send me information and or contact me about the following programs.

____Becoming a High Achiever
____Making Your Life & Career Work
____Managing the Change Process
____Other (Please describe your interest)

Name_____

Company_____

Address_____

_____

_____

Office Phone_____

Note. If you are interested in one of our programs for your Company or organization and are not directly responsible for decisions with respect to training and development, you might want to ask the responsible officer to contact us directly. If you would like us to contact this person, please indicate whether or not you feel it would be appropriate for us to use your name in making the contact: YES NO (circle one)

Person to Contact _____

Position_____

Address (if different from above)_____

_____

_____

Phone _____

FOLD & STAPLE